T. Psychic Soldier

THE TRUE STORY OF ONE MAN'S PSYCHIC JOURNEY
FROM CHILDHOOD TO THE SAS AND BEYOND...

by
Bob Curry

ISBN-13: 9781499798883
ISBN-10: 1499798881

Library of Congress Control Number: 2014911492
CreateSpace Independent Publishing Platform
North Charleston, South Carolina

Dedicated to Nicola,
My Shining Star.
Love and Light.

Poems

GLOSSARY

2IC	Second in Command
AMFL Battalion	Ace Mobile Force Land
AR-15	5.56 rifle, Vietnam era
Blow	To blow up (set off explosives)
Bergen	Backpack
Badged	Made a serving member of the regiment (22 SAS)
Bashers	Improvised shelters
BV	Artic vehicle mainly used by Royal Marines
CO	Commanding Officer
DPM	Disruptive Pattern Material
DS Training Staff	Directing Training Staff
DZ	Drop Zone (parachute insertion), for men or equipment
FUP	Forming Up Point (prior to an assault on a position)
GPMG	General Purpose Machine Gun, 7.62, belt fed
HF Radio	High-Frequency Radio
H & K	Heckler and Koch MP5 submachine gun
LP	Landing Point (helicopter)
MID	Mentioned in Despatches
NCO	Non-Commissioned Officer

NAAFI	Navy Army Air Force Institute
NATO	North Atlantic Treaty Organisation
OC	Officer Commanding
OP	Observation Post
PNG	Passive Night Vision Goggles
QGM	Queens Gallantry Medal
REME	Royal Electrical and Mechanical Engineers
RMP	Royal Military Police
Recce	Reconnaissance
RV	Rendezvous
RSM	Regimental Sargent Major
RTU	Returned to Unit
RPG Sevens	Russian shoulder-Fired lightweight grenade launchers
SLR	Self-Loading Rifle, 7.62
SSM	Squadron Sargent Major
SMG	Sub-Machine Gun
SOP	Standard Operating Procedures
Trig Point	Triangulation pillar used in map reading and surveying

INTRODUCTION

I used to be the biggest sceptic with regards to people saying that they were mediums who could contact the spirit world. I will try and answer concerns that you might have about passing and what happens to your loved ones who have gone before you.

And I will tell you why I believe that we are all spirit people having an earthly experience and that we do not die but simply return to the spirit world.

Why do I believe this? The answer to that is simple: I class myself as a fairly normal person, taking into consideration my life's journey, and I have come into contact with spirit people from time to time like many of you will. Why? Because they are with us. I also communicate with them on a daily basis at my studio when I am giving one-to-one readings to people, and when I stand on a platform and bring loved ones through for audiences, giving evidence of survival in the spirit world and proving we don't die; we simply go back to where we came from, the spirit world.

Every situation in this book is true. There is no fiction, and I was personally a witness to the majority of events. I'm well aware of the opinions of many people who say, *When you're dead, you're dead.*

I strongly dispute that fact. I have seen spirits in full-body apparitions standing in front of me in broad daylight with no trickery or imagination on my part; also, I have seen spirits attempting to manifest themselves in front of me, once again in daylight, not at night. There were no shadows from lights or sunlight coming through windows making it look like something other than what it was. When you're standing in front of another person, you clearly know what you are looking at; it is a human body, and in this case one from the past, and I am sure without question that many of you would have been in this same situation and even more so if when you recognised the person that you were looking at as someone who you know passed to Spirit.

I was recently in Torquay, in the south of England. I was leaning on a wall overlooking the sea when I spotted two men wearing suits, carrying cloth-type briefcases. One had a leaflet in his hand, and they were heading towards me. They stopped, and the older one said, 'Hello. How are you? Can I give you this?' and he handed me a leaflet.

I replied, 'You're Jehovah's Witnesses, aren't you?'

Yes,' 'came the answer. I thanked him but indicated that it wasn't for me— his religion, that is. In response to this he asked, 'Why? What is your religion?' I answered 'spiritualist.'

'That isn't what the Bible says,' he replied.

'I see spirits and communicate with them. It doesn't get any clearer than that.'

He walked away without answering.

I wasn't being rude but merely expressing a point: everyone has their own beliefs, but mine is based on the evidence that I receive.

Introduction

My story begins with an extremely violent childhood, wherein daily beatings from my psychotic mother were the norm. She constantly told me that I was good for nothing, stupid, and a failure. I was to prove her wrong. As soon as I could, I left my so-called home and enlisted in the army at the age of fifteen and a half as a boy soldier. I joined the Royal Anglian Regiment and reached the rank of junior corporal. It was apparent that I had a flair for leadership. Two years later I joined the 1st Battalion, where I served for ten years, achieving the rank of sergeant and completing many intensive military courses with very good results. My leadership ability was confirmed. I found much of this time was served in Northern Ireland, where I saw a lot of active service, but I still needed a bigger challenge. So I moved on to reach my career ambition of passing selection for the 22 SAS Regiment. My ability was confirmed; I was not as my mother saw me. I had achieved the near impossible. The SAS have a saying: *'Many are called forward, but few are chosen. Who dares wins.'* And I had. I served in the SAS for the rest of my army career.

Spirits have always been with me, but I just wasn't fully aware of it. However, I would move on to realise this in later life, and it would become a part of my life—a big part.

I love working with spirits and am aware that certain parts of this book might come across as me being, I can only say, full of myself. This is not the case. I'm so pleased I can do this; it is the most enjoyable work I've ever done. I just love working with spirits, communicating from the spirit world to the earth plane, giving people undisputed evidence that I have their loved ones who have passed with me, telling them things that only they would know. How could I have known? I don't know these spirit people, and I never knew them on the earth's plane. It's a wonderful thing, and to think that mediumship was banned in this country at one time—what a loss that would have been, had the ban continued.

We should be joyful at the true medium who can bring the two worlds closer together and give hope to those of you who have unanswered questions, who are carrying guilt for not being there at the end of a person's life, and who want to know how they feel about this and many other things, all of which can be answered by the medium who is there for you.

Please look at my journey so far. How can you relate it to your own? I guarantee many of you can. However, I feel we should all live by the same principles: simple love and light.

1

MY JOURNEY BEGINS

My journey begins at a very young age. I had a small blue and white tricycle with the pedals on the front wheel and plastic streamers on the ends of the handlebars. I would pedal this around the back garden of the council house where we lived in Cambridge, England. It wasn't a big area, so I couldn't go far. It was a terraced house with a passageway in between the houses. This was around 1955, not long after the Second World War and rationing had ended.

My parents were both in the health service. My father was a male nurse and my mother an auxiliary nurse. Before they were married and knew each other my father was sent to Japan in the medical corps towards the end of the Second World War, and my mother by her own admission had a good time, as she was only twenty when the war started and was fond of pilots: American for chocolate and nylons, etc., and RAF for good times in officers' messes and dance halls. This continued until the end of the war, when reality struck home hard.

My father returned to the UK and was promised a new start and a good life to come. As the aggressors had been defeated, the country was to be rebuilt and become a land of milk and honey. Well, as you know from the history books, this was not the case; poverty ruled.

On his return from Japan my father found work at a hospital not far from his mother's house, where he lived with his parents and brother and also three sisters. My mother was working at the same hospital. This was how they met. The year was probably 1947 or '48. I know my mother did not go down well with my father's family, as I believe they felt she was not good enough for him.

She had a brother who was in the services, as most people were at the time. She said that when he returned to England and found out what she had been up to during the war years, while he had been out fighting for king and country, he chased her around the house with a knife, trying to kill her. She must have got away.

A marriage followed, and in 1951 my eldest brother arrived. I've been told my mother had a girl after that, but unfortunately she went back to the spirit world. Apparently my mother could not get over this, and in 1953 along I came, which was to her great disappointment, as I was not a girl, and for that fact I would pay for the rest of her life.

There was a brick shed in the garden of our house. Every house had one the same: two doors, one on the left, one on the right. The right-hand one, as you walked through it, had on the right-hand side a coal bunker and an area divided off by three planks of wood that you would slide into grooves on either end of the wall, one on top of the other. This would divide up an area where you could store coal, which was delivered once a year, and I remember my mother standing by the shed door, counting the sacks of coal that went into what she called the coal bunker. I remember her saying that you couldn't trust anyone—they'd rip you off—thus throwing in doubt the honesty of the delivery drivers. This showed her frame of mind at the time. Everyone was trying to do it to her—I mean rob her, get one over on her—and she was constantly alert and defensive. I suppose a lot of that rubbed off on me, as whenever I sit in cafés and restaurants, it's always in a corner, with my back to the wall. It has become a habit. If I arrange to meet friends in one of these places and they know me well, when they come in they will always look in the corner seats where they know I'll be, constantly on the defensive.

On the other side of the shed there were garden tools and a cobbler's hobbling iron. This was a device that was used to repair shoes, allowing the leather soles to be removed and new pieces of leather placed over them and cut to size around the perimeter of the shoe. This I witnessed my father do on many occasions. In those days you did all your own repairs, including darning socks, sewing buttons on shirts, putting patches on clothes, and anything else that needed doing.

Hanging up in this shed was a fur-lined flying suit. It was a one-piece lined with sheepskin from top to bottom, along with a type of gabardine material. It had many zip pockets on the outside. It had clearly been used for air crew in the Second World War, as they flew at high altitudes with large, gaping holes in the sides of the aircraft, where machine guns would point out. It looked very warm. However, you would not have walked far wearing it before being covered in sweat, however ideal for the job it was.

My father would wear this suit to go to work on the back of his friend's motorbike on occasions. I remember him doing this: no crash helmet, no gloves, just a flying suit. His friend worked at the same hospital as him, and I can recall him going on the back of this motorcycle even in the snow. I understand he came off it once, and I think his friend broke some bones.

3

I remember I used to have a dream, repeated most nights, about this flying suit. In the dream I would be upstairs on the landing, which was covered in lino, a cheap floor covering that you could get at the time, as all floors upstairs were bare boards, and downstairs covered in a black bitumen material. In the dream I would only be wearing socks on my feet, and I would be pulled towards a bedroom door that was on the end of the landing. This was my eldest brother's bedroom. I would slide along the landing but I couldn't get traction to stop myself. I would slide towards the door and hit it with my feet sideways. The door would burst open, and there would be a man wearing the flying suit, who would turn to look at me as I came through the door, and as I only had socks on and couldn't get traction to run out of the room, at this point I would always wake up.

This dream has come to me until recently, when it seems to have stopped. I have many theories as to why I have this dream. One of them is that maybe someone had passed in that suit during the war. I know that this was an instance of spirits working with me at a very young age. This was my first contact with spirits, or my first awareness of them.

This dream left me not wanting to go up the stairs in case I saw the man, and this caused a problem, as the only toilet we had was at the top of the stairs, near this room. So I would hold myself as long as I could before going up the stairs. Sometimes it was too late, and I would have an accident in my shorts, giving my mother an excuse to take her frustrations out on me physically. And I would be presented with a bucket of water and soap and ordered to wash them by hand—remember, I was only three or four years old.

Can you imagine presenting a three- or four-year-old in this present day and age with a bucket of water and soap, and standing over them making them wash underpants out of this bucket? I would like to think that social services would be straight on the case. To my mother it wouldn't matter who was there, other children or my brother; this task would have to be carried out.

And not only that, there was a reason, a very good reason, why these accidents happened, but how does a child of that age explain to a psychotic mother about the man in the flying suit? This would have just ended up with another beating, this time for telling lies.

I know what it's like for a child to be abused and not be able to turn to anyone who is going to believe him. *Why do you make things up? Why do you tell lies and try and get people into trouble?* This is all he would have been told. I feel really sorry for children in that situation today, of which I'm sure there are many. You understand when you're older that you weren't planned; you were just an accident that had to be put up with, unfortunately for you.

I remember the '50s as being dark days. We were just getting over a world war, and there was a threat of nuclear war with Russia, and various other conflicts were happening around the world. Television had only been invented for the average person in black and white with two channels, ITV and BBC. That was your lot, and of course the test card, showing a picture of a little girl, is one of the things I remember to this day.

Drink also played a part with my parents as I grew up. I'm not saying they drank on a daily basis, but when there would be family get-togethers at different family members' houses, drink was the main theme. I remember one such gathering at my house. It went on to the very, very early hours, and the next day my eldest brother and I were going round looking at all the bottles and the glasses and the mess, and making up and testing drinks—not good. I think everybody had brought along with them a bottle, or as it was in those days, a crate of beer as well. Anyway, it was some get-together, and they were clearly paying for it the next day. This was the only relief I got from my mother, as she wouldn't dare assault me in front of the relatives.

There is no doubt about it that drink causes trouble. You don't see people walking around falling over and assaulting others in normal daylight, but at night when drink is involved and the werewolves come out in these people. I guarantee that the majority of people that are in prison today are there through drink-related acts.

I'm not trying to preach. I'm just pointing out the obvious, and not only that, as these are things that I have learnt in my life, sometimes by the mistakes of others and sometimes by my own. None of us are perfect. We all have skeletons in the cupboard, just some worse than others.

My life was not good at home. I would receive severe beatings from my mother every day without fail. These would include the use of her fists, feet, head butts, and any implement of punishment she could get hold of, as well as well-placed kicks to the genitals and savage hair pulling, which she used to swing me around so that she could get to other parts of my body. I recall a time when she punched me straight in the nose really hard for no reason. Blood flew out of my face uncontrollably. I was sure she had broken my nose. She just looked at me and said, 'Don't be so stupid. Put your head back.' I remember lying on the settee on my back with my head over the end, pinching the top of my nose to stop the bleeding and nearly choking on the blood—motherly love.

We also had an airing cupboard in our kitchen. Every house had one. It was for airing clothes. There were four shelves made up of wooden rods probably 12.5 millimeters thick. She broke every one of these rods on me. There must have been at least forty on the shelves. It was clear that she missed the Texas ranches and millionaire's life she had been promised by the fast-talking GIs.

Mealtime wasn't any better. I couldn't eat brussels sprouts or cauliflower; I just couldn't swallow them. They wouldn't go down but came straight back up, and I paid for this every mealtime when they were on the menu. I would have to sit there until I ate them. This would go on for hours. She would walk behind me like some possessed rottweiler. I remember her words: 'You will not leave that table until you've eaten them.' I never did eat them. I knew it would just end in another beating when her patience ran out.

Homework was fun. I had to do it in the living room. She was a self-appointed teacher with a ruler in her hand, and if my writing wasn't tidy enough for her, she would grab my hand and hit me across the knuckles hard with this ruler. If I spelt the word wrong or couldn't do my tables, the same punishment would fall upon me.

Primary-school photograph of Bob at five years old.
Looking at this photograph, there is no indication of the
abuse that he is suffering at home at the hands of his
mother. A very worried young child full of innocence to this
world. All he wanted was to be loved like other children;
however, this was not the case.

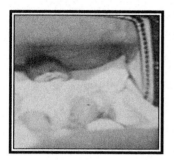

Bob as a baby. He was not a girl, much to his mother's disgust.

Bob (right) with his brother at their first home in Russell Street, Cambridge.

Bob (left) and his brother sat in a wheelbarrow at their home in Cherry Hinton, Cambridge. All the back gardens were the same, as you can see in the background. The path would be run up and down many times after school on shopping trips for Bob's mother, and if the fifteen-minute time allowance wasn't kept, then punishment would await his return. The shop was in the village, some distance away—rarely, if ever, was the time achieved.

Spirit in the Sky

Spirit in the sky, please tell me why life was so different from the rest,
never blessed.
No love for me today, you're not going out to play, and keep them hooli-
gan kids away.

We were better than them all. Who was the fool
You better be home from school on time.
There's shopping to be done, and make sure you run there and back.
Don't test my patience today, or you'll pay in the usual way.

Sticks and stones broke my bones and names always hurt me.
Dreams of a better place and a kinder member of the human race to take
the place
so there would be no tears for me today, no blood to wipe away.
Love would be a dream too soon.
I might as well have tried to fly to the moon.

Life has been hard for me because I was always told I'm useless, you see,
and I'd never make anything of it.
What I would like to dispute that fact, when I look back.

There's nothing left to say, except never treat a child in that way, and I pray.

Spirit in the sky, please tell me why.

2

MY SCHOOL DAYS

School days were not good. I found school very boring, and I knew from a young age that I wanted more than just sitting around in a classroom being told what to do by an ageing schoolmistress, as many of them were in those days. We lived very much in the Victorian days as far as education was concerned. There was no possibility of not doing the work, as you'd soon get a ruler rapt across your knuckles if you didn't. That was their way of teaching: knock it into you.

As we all know, this simply does not work. You can't make anyone do anything they don't want to; you have to make them want to do it, and the only way to achieve this is by kindness and your personality. I've learnt this all my life, whether instructing in the military or training locksmiths in the locksmith training company that I own.

Home life was not good. My psychotic mother was on the rampage every day. As soon as she saw me it would be an excuse for a beating. It often got out of hand, and I didn't want to be there. I remember walking home from school one lunchtime, wishing that there would be people waiting there saying there had been a mistake: *You don't live here. You have to come with us.* I was seven at the time. All of this continued up to when I left school. My school days were not good. Infant and junior school were very much the same. However, when I got into my last two years of junior school, it had become very violent. Fighting was the norm.

The secondary school I attended was Netherhall Secondary Modern, Cambridge. This school was divided up—boys one side, girls the other, and never the two to meet. I found it hard work. So-called playtimes meant dodging bullies in the playground, which there were many of. Fighting was an everyday event punishable by the cane from the headmaster. That meant the defendant and the aggressor. No trial. You were both guilty.

Every teacher had an implement of punishment at hand. They enjoyed punishing the kids at every opportunity, and even if one didn't arise, they would invent one so they could hit us.

The science teacher had a knot in the rubber pipe of his Bunsen burner to punish us with. The deputy headmaster had a custom-made sole of a shoe with some writing on it explaining the meaning of punishment. The metalwork teacher had a half-meter steel ruler. Our gym teachers were the worst; we would have to strip off our clothes and run through a line of cold showers on both sides of a wall, entering at one end and exiting at the other, to be met by two teachers who were each armed with the sole of a plimsoll, and every boy would be whacked across the wet, bare backside by one or the other. All the time they were laughing at what they were doing; this was paedophile behaviour.

All the other teachers used blackboard rulers about one meter long to punish us, delivered across the backside, and our headmaster had a wardrobe full of canes, from very thin to very thick. Which one you received was chosen on merit for the so-called crime that you had allegedly committed, and I say 'allegedly' because you never had a say in your defence; you were just punished for no reason. No democracy in this school. You were ruled by dictators who had a free hand in dishing out the punishment.

My mother would visit my form teacher after school hours. These meetings would take place in my classroom. This happened in my final year at school, supposedly to discuss my education. However, my teacher was ex-RAF air crew, World War II, and the fact that these meetings went on for hours and every classroom had a stock cupboard at the back of it, where others had been caught in compromising situations, didn't leave much to the imagination.

Permission was given by my mother to my form teacher to punish me if and when he felt like it. This was confirmed to me by my form master, who tried to carry this out. I was fifteen and had had enough of this treatment. I was told to stay behind one day after class. The teacher told me to stand at his desk at the front of the classroom, he then produced a cane about half a meter long, with very big notches in it, and said to me, 'Bend over, boy.' He started to poke me in the chest with his finger. I was about to snap. I looked him straight in the eyes and said, 'You aren't hitting me with that.' Still poking me, he said that my mother had said that he could punish me if and when he felt fit.

I said again, 'You are not hitting me with that.' He looked into my eyes and knew what was coming next, so he said, 'Get out, boy,' and I walked away from this bully with pride. I had stood up to him, only in self-defence. Had it come to physical self-defence, I could not have won, as I would have been sent to borstal (a young offenders institute) for hitting a teacher, no matter what the circumstances. That's how it was in those days, and young offenders institutes in those days were everybody's idea of hell. These establishments were run on the lines of national service. It was all discipline and more discipline. There was no way out—unlike the prison life that we see on the television today.

Thank god for social services. Where were they then? If this behaviour took place now, all of these people would be serving long jail sentences, and rightly deserved. We were the victims, but no one would listen to us. I know how it feels to be an abused child. It stays with you for the rest of your life, and I use the word 'scarred' because this is what I am. However, we learn to live with it and get on with our lives. It is in the past, like World War II. It must never happen again.

Taking into consideration all of this treatment and listening to the youth of today and the reasons they commit crime, it is a wonder that I am not a complete psychopath with the way I was treated. I just feel that we have to deal with it in our own ways and get on with life and learn not to treat people in the same way. It simply doesn't work.

My friends were not allowed to come around to my house. My mother said they were hooligans and lowlifes. Well, you couldn't get much lower than we were. At least they had a home and didn't get beaten. I used to get out of the house at every opportunity I could. I would go fishing in the season as much as I could. It wasn't to catch fish; it was to get away. I had a methylated spirit cooker, and I would cook breakfast on the side of the river bank, much to the amusement of my friends who had sandwiches made for them by their mothers.

I would have an egg, a slice of bacon, a couple of pieces of bread, and a small Billy can for cooking. I even made my own tea, which always tasted better outside. It was obvious it was the outdoor life for me. This would come in handy in my future career. I learned a lot from these little fishing trips—not only fishing, but simple cooking.

Another interest that my friends and I had was air rifles. We were very careful with them. Safety seemed to be the main point all the time, and we never did anything stupid. There was an old quarry where I lived in Cambridge. We would go there and put up cans and anything else that would fall over if hit by an air rifle pellet.

My friends and I became very good shots, and I must admit I stood out from the rest. It was as if I had a flair for shooting. You had to be fourteen to own an air rifle in those days and accompanied by someone over seventeen. We never had anyone over seventeen with us, so we would wrap the air rifle up in cloth, tie it around the crossbar of a bicycle, and put a fishing landing net in the front basket, which made it look like we were going fishing. Otherwise we would have been stopped by the police, and this would have meant confiscation of our beloved air rifles and a beating from both my father for bringing the police to the door and my psychotic mother for good measure—also, a court appearance, and of course another beating when I got home.

I paid for my rifle with money I had saved from my paper round. I bought it from a friend. It only cost a couple of pounds. Air rifles were plentiful. Secondhand shops where you could buy them were appearing everywhere. A top-of-the-range was only five pounds.

No one knew I had it. I used to keep it in my friend's shed. We always used to get our pellets from an old cobbler shop in the village. The owner knew we were underage, but he also knew we were responsible, so he sold us the pellets. He used to call us 'you old boys,' meaning youngsters.

We would also go fishing. We weren't very good, and if we caught any-thing at all it was by some miracle. Dads didn't take their kids fishing in those days. 'Children are to be seen and not heard'—that was the saying. But I liked it anyway, as it got me away from the house and the violence that went with it. I still like the peace and quiet on river banks, and how if you watch you will see river-bank life moving around, like rabbits playing in fields, or, if you're very quiet, a fox coming along.

Obviously I would tell my mother that I had gone fishing whenever my whereabouts were requested.

Another interest I had was the Sea Cadets which I was a member of for at least two years. I had an interest in joining the navy and I wanted to see the world. I remember reading a book called *Robinson Crusoe*, by Daniel Defoe. I used to look at this book and see how he lived on his desert is-land, and I used to think to myself that I'd love to do that. I could quite easily live like that. Maybe it was the loner in me coming out. Or was it the wanting of a better life?

I ran away from home once. I took with me all the basic equipment I would need: sewing kit, washing kit, fire-lighting material, a good pen-knife that I owned, my trusty air rifle, and lots of pellets. I'd had enough. I was going off to live in the woods. Unfortunately, it didn't last long. My lovely mother realised I was missing, so she phoned the police to come and look for me, and she said to them, 'Make sure you take a big dog with you. He hates dogs.'

There was a lot of woodland in the area where I lived. I knew of a cave where I could hide. It was up high, out of the weather and the elements, and had good observation. A fire would have been out of the question, as the smoke would have been seen from a distance. Anyway, I was in the cave, and had collected branches that I had cut some distance away from the cave, and brought them there to cover the entrance of the cave. Not being naive, I knew that if there were wood cut in the vicinity, it would lead them to my hide.

I wasn't there long when I heard a dog. I looked through my camouflage and saw a policeman with a police dog on a lead. They went straight past me. My plan had worked. However, I knew they wouldn't give up, and clearly they didn't have local knowledge. I had to weigh up my options: Would I sneak back, put everything back in its place, and deny going anywhere? Or would I carry on and properly get found by the police, and then be treated harshly and not listened to, even if I then explained why I had done this? The danger was that I might be put in a home, which was not a good option in those days, as we know from news events concerning the activities carried out by adults against children in those establishments during that period of time and people now being charged with abuse against children and young adults. Would I take the risk? It was now dark. I was comfortable and quite happy to stay there through the night and move on the next day. However, because the police were involved, it was inevitable I'd be caught before long, so I made the decision to return home. I had to get everything back in its place and deny that I had ever been anywhere.

So I did. I sneaked back, concealed my equipment in the shed, and walked into the house like nothing had happened. When asked, and I quote, 'Where the hell have you been? The police are out looking for you and they've got dogs,' I said 'Why?' and explained I'd been somewhere quite innocent. The police turned up and my mother told them I was back, obviously frightened of the dark, and that she would deal with it. I knew what that meant, and I wasn't frightened of the dark; as I said, it was the consequences that came with being caught that concerned me most.

Anyway, my time in the Sea Cadets was fun. In the summer we would take out a boat called an eight, which was owned by the unit. We would row this up and down the River Cam, which is the main river running through Cambridge, with an ageing captain at the helm shouting out the orders, trying to get us to row in sequence. I don't think it ever happened, but it was a laugh to young boys and girls. I don't think we took it too seriously, to the annoyance of this captain who I'm sure had commanded bigger vessels in his time.

Yes, we had fun. We were treated like we were in the navy while at this 'shore ship,' as the navy called it; every establishment that was connected to the Royal Navy that didn't float was called a ship. Yes, we had good times, until a trip was arranged to go to HMS Ganges, a shore-based training establishment on the coast. This was to see what the navy was all about. Most of us that were in my unit went, including the girls, and I was glad that I went on this trip, as it showed me what life in the navy was really like. They were very much steeped in tradition from back when Lord Nelson ruled the waves.

The accommodation was terrible, the food was worse, and no one seemed happy. Everyone was covered in spots;. This was not for me. How could I go from what I was going through to this? We returned on Saturday to Cambridge and had a parade Monday night, where I brought all my kit along, washed and ironed by myself, and handed in my resignation. That was the end of my navy career. Obviously I don't want to cast the Royal Navy in a bad light. I know now for sure that a lot has changed for the better: you can't treat people that way anymore, and the accommodation and food has greatly improved. It's like everything else: they had to modernise.

Bob wearing his Sea Cadet uniform in the back garden of the house in Cherry Hinton, Cambridge. The plan was to escape to the Royal Navy. However, the trip to HMS Ganges saved the day, and a more beneficial trip would be made to the army, followed by a career. Spirits were clearly working on Bob's side at this time. A move from the family to the correct career.

3

SCHOOL TRIP TO THE ARMY

Soon after I went on a school trip to the army at Bury St Edmunds, the depot for the Royal Anglian Regiment. We had a great day. We all got issued a pair of overalls, went over the assault course, fired rifles and machine guns on the range, and got fed all we wanted to eat. At tea-time I had a cream cake. I couldn't believe it. What a change. This wasn't the navy; this was ten thousand times better. I knew where my career lay. I'd been shown. Was Spirit with me again? I think so, and now I'm sure that this has been the case all through my life: I'm guided by spirits to the right things to do. However, and I'm sure you will agree, we have to listen to what's guiding us, and this we don't always do.

Unfortunately, my day trip to the army was ruined by arriving home at 1715 hours—not good. My mother had forgotten that I was visiting the army. I was greeted by, 'Where the hell have you been? What time do you call this? There was shopping to do. Now we've got nothing in the house.'

I tried to explain that I had told her I was going on a school trip to the army, but she denied all knowledge of this, and as an attempt at punishment she said there was no tea—I should've been there before. Unfortunately, I said to my peril, 'I've had tea with the army,' and then my biggest mistake—I said, 'And we also had a cream cake.' I hit the wall backwards, hard. I had been punched in the face and then descended upon by a raving lunatic, punches flying everywhere, kicking, hair tearing. Then, not satisfied with her efforts, she picked up a pair of steel washing tongs. These were massive and heavy. I was in the corner on the floor, now defenceless. All I could do was try and cover up my body with my arms. As she brought down the washing tongs to my head, I raised my arm to stop the blow and it connected with the tongs. The pain was unreal. My arm fell limp and useless, but it stopped the blow.

She came at me again, and now I only had one arm. In a pathetic attempt to defend myself and I'm sure save my life, I managed one feeble strike back, which connected with her mouth. Blood flew out—big mistake. I knew no more. Then my lights went out.

I don't know what happened. I must have been unconscious, but I don't know for how long. All I can remember is crawling up the hall and up the stairs one step at a time, not really knowing where I was. My arms were in agony. I hurt in every part of my body. I had lumps all over my face, my head hair was missing, and I was bleeding. It was like I'd been set upon by a pack of lunatics, not just one person. She had unbelievable strength. They say that the mentally ill have the strength of ten men, and that they take some holding down—well, I can confirm that. I lay on my bed in agony. I don't know how long I was there. All I remember hearing was my father shouting my name at the bottom of the stairs. I managed to get off my bed and went to the top of the stairs. I must have looked a mess, covered in blood and bruises, clothes ripped and torn.

I was by now beside myself with anger. I shouted at him, 'Don't you start! Ask her what she did to me.' He looked at me and I'm sure he could see the state I was in. I expected an assault up the stairs and a beating from one end of the house to the other, but no. It was obvious to him, I'm sure, that I was the defendant and she the aggressor. It is still hard for me to go back to those days, even though I'm putting them in writing, to live through them again—not good.

I was desperate to leave that house. How could anyone treat a child in that way? I have talked to others who were around my age at that time, and it is clear that this situation was not uncommon in other households—however, probably not to this extreme.

Eventually we moved from this house to a brand-new one on the other side of town, on the North Arbury estate. The night before we moved, the house caught fire. The chimney pot went up in flames. They were leaping out of the top, smoke everywhere. The fire brigade was called and had to put a canvas over the mantelpiece and put the fire hose down the chimney to put the fire out to stop the rest of the house going up in flames. If it had gone up, so would have the three other attached houses. This was the final act of hate from that house. I was glad to move. There were so many bad memories there.

I was recently talking to one of my aunts and told her what had happened in our house and how my mother had been. My aunt was amazed and said she had no knowledge of this—well, no, she wouldn't have. This was all done behind closed doors, most of the time when my father was not there, which resulted in fifteen and a half years of hell.

I would remember that school trip. Spirit was there working for me, I'm convinced. *This is your way out*, I was being told. Spirit was taking me there and showing me. *Now go.* And I did, and how glad I was—at the beginning, anyway. I thought, *No more lunatic, no more beatings.* How wrong I was. I wouldn't get rid of her that easy. I still had a heavy price to pay, and pay I would, for many years to come.

4

ARMY LIFE

Blenheim Camp, Bury St Edmonds, Suffolk Depot, the Royal Anglian Regiment, 1968

It was August 1968. My school days would soon come to an end. I was fifteen and a half and allowed to leave school. In those days you had no choice: you were out—no staying on, no studying for exams. You were out.

I'd been to the army recruiting office to join up. I could enlist as a boy soldier, known as a junior entrant, with my parent's permission, so my father signed the papers. The recruiting sergeant asked me where I wanted to go and what unit I wanted to be in. My education wasn't good and there weren't many choices. It was the infantry or nothing, I was told. I said that I wanted to join the Royal Anglian Regiment, as I'd been to their depot on a school trip. The sergeant said that he couldn't guarantee it. I told him that my eldest brother was in the Coldstream Guards, so he wrote it down as a second choice. Once again Spirit was looking after me, as he didn't send me to the Coldstream Guards. At the time this would have been hell. I would have been from one situation to another. Thank you, Spirit. You saved me. I went to the Royal Anglian Regiment at Bury St Edmonds, Suffolk, a county regiment for local people, which was much better and more relaxed.

I remember my father giving me a haircut before I went, and I must've looked ridiculous. It was short in the back and on the sides, and the final act of humiliating me. I arrived at the depot, the start of my army career. How surprised I was at the lenient way we were all treated. We were shown how to do things without being shouted at. This was completely the opposite of what my brother was suffering in the Coldstream Guards.

The first night in the army was great. I had a clean bed of my own and had been fed three times that day, and I'd had a cream cake for tea and no beating from my mother. It just couldn't get better.

All the others in my accommodation, which was a wooden hut holding thirty-two people, with a coke fire at both ends, were crying for their mums. They'd realised they'd made a big mistake and should have taken that job at the baker's shop or the café, as they had been offered. It was clear the army was not for them.

The coke for our fires was rationed, there was no central heating, it was freezing at night, and we always ran out of coke, so this led to clandestine raids on the coke yard. With our coke scuttles at the ready, we would scale the brick perimeter wall, get under the three strands of barbed wire, fill up our coke scuttles, hand them back over the wall to our accomplices on the other side, and return to our huts, the heroes of the night, never to get caught and never to be found out.

It was 0630 hours and the lights came on. We were all told to get up and wash and shave. Not a problem for me. I was at the paper shop at 0630 every day to do my paper round—all this with no alarm clock. Easy.

It was like starting any other job. You assess everyone else, trying to work out who are the good guys and who are the bad ones. I was always very good at reading people from a very young age. This was my psychic side, which was helpful because I knew who to recognise—who the bullies were and who the weak ones were. I suppose I've always been a defender of the weak, bullies would come from other huts and try and pick on us, as we were the new boys. It was suggested that the way to stop this was to join the boxing team. No one in his right mind picked on the boxing team. I was very good at boxing, and the bullies knew not to come in our hut, as two of us were in the boxing team.

I had a friend. Barney was his name. I remember he came from Northampton, and he was in the boxing team. One day when a bully turned up looking for money and anything else he could get, he started on Barney. Big mistake. Barney hit him once with a very good right hand, which sent the assailant to the ground, not to get up. He was carried out of the hut and to the MI room. This was a medical centre. He was taken to hospital, and we found out some weeks later that he had been discharged from the army with head injuries. His bullying days were over.

We found a way to deal with the bullies, some a lot older than us, who came from other huts to pick on us. What we would do was send a rec-ce out in the daytime to find out where they slept in the huts—which beds were theirs—and we would count how many beds down from the door the bullies slept in and was, it on the left or on the right side of the room. To ensure we had the right bed the bully had to be lying on it or his possessions would be around it, everything military had to have your name on, we were then set for a night time raid..

After bed check, which was done every night by the duty NCO, and when all the lights were out and people were asleep, we would put our boots in a pillowcase. These were our marching boots. They were made of leather and had studs in the steel-tipped toes and heels very heavy. We would sneak to the bullies' hut, open the door quietly, and sneak in, counting the beds down the side. The bully slept until we got to him. He would then receive many blows from these pillowcases all over his body, anywhere we could hit him. It was the job of the last man through the door on the way in to pick up the fire bucket with water in it, and as we withdrew from the assault he would throw the water and the bucket over the bully. This ensured he would have to pay for his mattress, which would be ruined.

When I look back, I know Spirit has always been with me. There have been many times in my life when I have had near misses and nearly been sent back to the spirit world. I have been saved by my guide, who is a North American Indian called Bold Eagle. I believe we all have our spiritual journeys to follow. Sometimes we deviate from our paths, but generally we stay on the course.

I found army training easy. I liked being outside. Camping was a hobby. I got involved in outdoor activities as much as I could to get away from my mother. I took getting wet in my stride, so these were happy days for me. Marching was fun, and rifle drill. We spent a lot of time on the rifle ranges. I found that I was a very good shot, which I put down to my air rifle practice.

The NCOs—that is, the corporals and sergeants—were all very good to us. We were treated like humans, not screamed and shouted at. They had a laugh with us, and generally work was enjoyable. Drill was kept to the minimum. We didn't spend hours marching about the square like my brother did. We were a county regiment. Our emphasis was on training and becoming professional soldiers, which we did, and this training would most certainly save my life in the years to come.

Every weekday we had education to attend. We had to achieve our first, second, and third class certificates. These would take you up to the rank of warrant officer. First class was as high as a noncommissioned rank could go.

This was so much better than school. They actually cared about you and tried with you. I passed my third and second class certificates while I was there, CSE and O Level Standard. I could never have achieved that at school.

We didn't work weekends. Money was very short. We only earned three pounds a week, and out of this, one pound would go into your post-office savings book. Another pound would go into your credits, and you were given a pound to buy all your necessary daily items, like toothpaste, toothbrushes, boot polish, and Blanco Brasso. After that there was nothing left. This was the only downfall to being in the army. At that time you could earn more in civvy street, but never mind. I was fairly safe, especially from my psychotic mother.

One day I was sitting on a park bench under a streetlight in Bury St Edmonds, with my back to a large graveyard. I was sixteen at the time and had my girlfriend with me, of the same age. We were just talking. We had been seeing each other for a few weeks. Her parents had money. I was just a squaddie, not to be trusted. It was dark and late in the year. Leaves were on the ground and it was cold, but we didn't care, as there was nowhere else to go, and her house was definitely out of the question. Anyway, we were talking for a while when a strong smell started coming around us. I had not smelt this before. It was strange, very strange.

And then I heard someone or something walking through the leaves behind us. I jumped up. I looked through the railings of the graveyard to see who or what was coming towards us, but nothing was there, and the noise of walking in the leaves was so close it was nearly upon us.

I ran, and as I started off I noticed that my girlfriend was way ahead of me. I was so engrossed with what was happening that I hadn't noticed her running off. It was a fair way before we stopped. We were both fit, so it didn't bother us—the run, that is. When we did stop, I said, 'Did you hear something walking through the leaves?' I can't remember her answer, but I know it was obvious that she had. We never went there again.

To this day I don't know what it was, but I do know it was there.

My mother would not leave me alone. She found out that we did not work weekends, so she contacted me and said that if I did not come home at weekends, she would get the police to bring me home, and I would do as I was told until I was eighteen. I was devastated. I was only fifteen and a half at the time, and under my parents' control until eighteen, even though I was in the army. It wasn't worth it to test the situation, as if I'd come off worse, I may well have been discharged, and then what? I'd have to go home. The beatings would begin again.

I remember an open day at the depot. The Queen Mother was our colonel in chief, and she was to be presenting new colours to the regiment. All parents were invited. I remember my mother turning up in a fur coat, like she was somebody. However, this coat got her into the officers' mess tent with my father, who was wearing a suit, much to her pleasure, as she drank champagne all day and no doubt talked rubbish to the officers and their ladies or companions.

She was not happy when she found out that I was not being treated the same as my brother, who had joined the army two years before me, unfortunately with the Coldstream Guards, where discipline came first. I remember her telling me she had gone to visit him. He had been summoned to the guard room. He had had to march across, halt in front of them, and present himself. She thought this was fantastic. She could have been the Regimental Sargeant Major RSM. She would have loved it, screaming and shouting all day and physically assaulting the men. This was the norm in those days. It was made for her. She had missed her vocation in life.

Unfortunately, when she visited the depot at the Royal Anglian Regiment, things were different. We were a county regiment. Our priorities were not the same. Marching band drills were secondary to soldiering, which came first and which we were good at. This was the priority.

Anyway, she turned up at our camp and enquired at the guard room for me, expecting me to march across and salute, I am sure so she could see that I was under the thumb and being disciplined day and night. However, this was not the case. She was given a hut number to go to. I think it was number 37. This was the junior soldiers' wing. On arrival she walked into my hut, where everyone was lying on their beds except me. She couldn't believe it—no bull, just normal people. No one screaming out orders. I'm sure she was most disappointed, to say the least.

Because we were under sixteen, the army had to get permission from our parents if we wanted to smoke. This pleased my mother, as she received a form to say whether I could or not; obviously it returned with a no. She still had power in her hands. She could still control me. She knew the army had given her the upper hand. Life would carry on being unbearable. I would not be left alone. If I didn't contact her, she would write letters to see if I was still alive. She was concerned about me, obviously. This would annoy the army, and I would get it in the neck from them.

I remember the last beating I had from her. I was twenty-four. How sad is that? I was about to go on selection for the SAS. I was at my parent's house, against my will, and my father asked me what I was going to do with my army career. I said I was doing selection for the SAS. She jumped up and said, 'They won't take you. Who do you think you are?' and attacked me, grabbing my hair and punching me in the face. I was mad, very mad, but my father stood there and watched, not doing a thing to stop her—just standing behind, daring me to hit her. I knew this by the way he was looking at me. I asked him to get her off me. He did nothing. Eventually she released her grip on my hair. We had been taught unarmed combat in the army, so I had to use this to get her off me. It involved a hold on her wrist and a twist backwards, putting pressure at the same time on her thumb joint. This was done with my thumb. I could have followed up with several other moves that would have disabled her. However, I'd stopped the attack, so I left the house and that was that. I swore I was never coming back. They both needed help, serious medical help. In my eyes they were as bad as each other and deserved each other.

My two years were over as a boy solider. I'd had a good time, got promoted to corporal, and liked to instruct, which would set me in good stead for my future army career. I had learned to map read and was very good at weapon handling and range work. We had also spent a lot of time on exercise, honing our infantry skills—all good training for the future. I had also done a lot of adventure training. I was sent on an Outward Bound course at several civilian establishments in Ashburton, Devon. There I learnt the canoe in white water, abseiling, rock climbing, caving, hill walking, and many more skills. I enjoyed this, as I liked the outdoors.

But I was also sent on several military Outward Bound courses. They called them EL, standing for 'external leadership.' One of these was at Oswestry in Wales, and another at Fort William in Scotland. This particular course was in midwinter—preparation for Arctic warfare, I'm sure. I enjoyed this time. Yes, it was testing and hard work, but I was up for the challenge. A good thing about it was we were taught to pack our Bergens properly, with waterproof bags and even distribution of heavy items and everything inside—nothing hanging on the outside, like a hobo's bag, to ensure nothing was lost and no one could hear you coming. And one thing we had to do was take our letter home. This would be checked when we got back, to make sure we hadn't rubbished the countryside.

I liked sitting round the campfire on a starlit night, talking and singing. It was good fun. It's a pity that kids these days don't do more of this. We have the great outdoors to appreciate. We just need to get out there and see it. I still enjoy it to this day—maybe not running over the mountains with a large pack on my back, but certainly enjoying the views and appreciating what we have. There's something peaceful about being out there that takes the worries away from everyday life, as I'm sure many of you know who have outdoor pursuits, especially hill walking. To stand on the peak of a hill or mountain admiring the view and the peace and quiet! All you can see is a bird of prey soaring above you and all the hills and lakes in the distance. It's a wonderful place to be, especially to put your head right when you need to think.

It was time to join man service. First I had to complete eight weeks' training. I found this very easy, as everything we did I had already learnt over the last two years, so I sailed through with ease. On completion of the course we had a final party at the Bassingbourn barracks, just outside Cambridge. This had been a Second World War bomber base and was in exactly the same condition as it had been at that time. All the hangars on the air field and the runways are still there, all in good condition. These places were maintained by the Ministry of Defence, as they would be needed as before in case of another conflict. The depot had moved here from Bury St Edmunds about a year before.

About eight of us were in the navy army and air force institute NAAFI bar. I was with a very good friend of mine, Randolph Boyd from London. He drank rum and black and had several on the bar. The arrangement was to go to Bullock for a Chinese meal, but there was only one car. As everyone was leaving, Randy said, 'I'm not leaving these drinks on the bar,' so I said, 'I'll stay with you.' Spirit worked in more than one way that day and was with me without question.

Randy and I stayed there for the rest of the evening, talking over our two years as boy soldiers and now completing military training.. Randy was going to the Second Battalion and I was going to the First. This is where we were sent. Randy's battalion was in Belfast, and mine was in Londonderry. We were both going to see plenty of active service in Northern Ireland, and at the time didn't have a clue why.

The next day we heard the bad news. The lads who had gone for the Chinese had all crowded into one car, a Ford Anglia. As they were travelling to Buldock, there was a lorry trailer parked on top of a hill with no lights on. They obviously didn't see the trailer and went under the back of it at some speed. I think three were killed, and the others had horrific injuries. I would have been in that car.

We were all devastated—three of our training NCOs and four of our platoon either dead or very seriously injured. This was a blow like a hammer. How could this happen?

5

POSTED TO NORTHERN IRELAND

At this time the Royal Anglian Regiment was made up of three battalions and an additional company, known as the Tiger Company, who were in Gibraltar. The First Battalion was in Northern Ireland, and I was sent there. This was 1970. I was seventeen. I had to go to Londonderry, or 'Derry,' as it was known by the locals. I did not have any idea why I was there, but I was. On arrival at Ebrington Barracks, which was the naval base HMS Sea Eagle before the army took it over, there were very large white buildings with a drill square that doubled as a helicopter pad. To the front of it, overlooking the city of Londonderry, which looked normal like any other town in any other country, were people going about their normal daily business. However, there was the presence of flags flying from lampposts and the fact that curb stones were painted in different colours—red, white, and blue in Protestant areas, and green, white, and gold in Republican areas.

There was a religious war going on. This went back to William of Orange and the fact that the Republicans wanted a united Ireland and the Protestants didn't, and out in the middle of this was the police, and it was their job to keep the two apart and the army's job to aid the civil power—the police. And this is why I was there. Soldiers weren't allowed politics—just get on with the job.

I had to attend a two-week internal security training course at Ebrington Barracks, which was to prepare us for riots that were very common at the time, so they put us through realistic scenarios. On completion of this training I was sent to A Company, who were located in the city.

We loaded up a four-tonne lorry with all our equipment and drove out of the camp gate with a Land Rover in front of us. This Land Rover had three men in it who all had the SLR rifles. We drove down the hill, across the Craigavon Bridge, into the city, and finally to the Strand Road police station. As we went through the gate of the police station, the truck stopped and we climbed off of the back, and I was told, 'You're on patrol, Curry.' The only patrol I had ever done was in training, and with a rifle that was not carried by every soldier in Ireland at that time.

I was taken to two other soldiers, who were getting ready to go out through the gate. One said, 'Put your kit in this room, get your helmet, baton, shield, and attach your gas mask onto your belt, and come with us.' One of the men had a rifle, an SLR 7.62 mm with one empty magazine on it and one in his pouch on his belt, with ten rounds, but taped up with masking tape so he could not put a live magazine on his rifle by accident.

The other man, who was the patrol commander, had a radio on his belt and an aerial that looked like it was broken as it dragged on the floor. We went out of the gate, staying three to five metres apart so if we got shot at, it would not hit two of us.

We walked up the road to the Little Diamond and right into Williams Street, and then into the Bogside. The trouble began.

There was a group of maybe five youths on some waste ground, who instantly gave us abuse and then started throwing missiles at us. They were soon joined by others, and we were trapped and alone. Fifty became one hundred. We were in big trouble. The soldier who had the SLR took the tape off the magazine in his pouch, put it on his rifle, and cocked it, ready to fire.

Each soldier was issued a yellow card that stated the terms and conditions under which lethal force could be used. The main reason was your life being in danger, or others' lives or property that it was your duty to protect. After due warning, if you still feared that your life was in danger, you could then open fire with live ammunition. However, you had to get this right, because if you didn't and there was any doubt, you would be in deep trouble, firstly with the military and then of course in a civilian criminal court. It was clear that the rioters were aware of this. However, they were no more than ten feet away from us.

It was a mad crowd of one hundred plus, all throwing anything they could get to injure or kill us. The patrol commander, who was a private solider just like me, got on the radio and told the company HQ what was going on, to be told 'Stop exaggerating.' He said again what was happening and had the same reply. The officer in charge, called the company commander, was for some wild reason convinced we were playing games. A lot of officers who were in the forces at this time were there through tradition. Their fathers and their grandfathers had often been in the same regiment, so they'd had to follow the family line. Whether they were any good or not, or capable enough, didn't matter. They were in, and it was clear some of them resented being there, mixing with the lower ranks and living in very substandard accommodations.

I could not believe that the radio, which should never had worked where it was, did. It was a very old A40 with a half-mile range over open ground. Spirit was there for me, I'm convinced, as the company commander sent a patrol to see 'what all the fuss was about,' we were told later.

This patrol came round the corner into Williams Street and saw the crowd that had us trapped, which was now about five hundred strong. The only reason we were still alive was the fact that we had a rifle loaded, and not one of them wanted to be the first to get shot.

The whole of A Company, which I was part of, was deployed to rescue us. So was C Company and Support Company and B Company. It was a war zone. This battle went on for two days and nights. Other units across Northern Ireland were called in to assist. We came under fire from .45 Thompson submachine guns, M1 carbines, Garan rifles that fired armour-piercing rounds, and an assortment of other weapons, sometimes handguns at close range. We were bombarded with petrol bombs, blast bombs, and nail bombs constantly for the complete period that I can only describe as a battle. I've never seen so much anger. I didn't even know why I was there. The party line was, 'To assist the civil powers in maintaining the peace.' Welcome to Northern Ireland, Bob.

Gallantry Medals should have been awarded that day to the three of us, as we held our ground despite overwhelming numbers against us, and we only had small tin shields to protect ourselves. There was also the fact that not one of us was over eighteen years old. I am convinced that Spirit made that radio work and also told the OC to send a patrol to see what

was going on. I think as well that we showed great restraint in not opening fire even though we were well within our rights to do so. However, I
am sure that this would have brought certain death to the three of us, as
in the situation in Iraq where those poor RMPs were trapped in that police station with very little ammunition to protect themselves. After they
were attacked by a massive crowd, the ammunition was soon expended,
and death followed shortly after.

This tour lasted two years, and there were many more near-death situations that I found myself in. It just seemed like every time I went out on
patrol, someone tried to kill me. We just didn't have the equipment to
deal with the situation. We found ourselves in inadequate vehicles. It was
like a government was trying to run itself on a shoestring. For protection from fragmentation devices we were issued with flak jackets, which
were purchased from the Americans secondhand from the Vietnam War.
They were next to useless in comparison with those that are issued to
our troops today in Afghanistan. At least these new ones stop bullets,
but there was no Gore-Tex clothing, no waterproof boots—and anyone
that has been to Northern Ireland knows how it rains. It's not called the
Emerald Isle for nothing. We were also desperately short of manpower.
We worked twenty-eight days on, two days off—when you were on duty,
that is. You would work two hours on patrol, two hours protection in tow-
ers, and, if really unlucky, - the cook house.. Despite any sleep you could
get during these periods, which might be an hour here and there in between these tasks, you were still exhausted at the end of twenty-eight
days.

On your two days back in camp, you would have to maintain your vehicles
and weapons, exchange damaged equipment—which was plentiful, due
to the constant abuse it received from the aggressors—laundry uniforms,
and pack everything back up, ready to go again. I remember I used to look

forward to visiting the NAAFI in Ebrington Barracks, which was run by local civilians. I would buy a crispy bacon roll and a pint of ice-cold Harp lager.

The Battle of Bligh's Lane

It was a Sunday. I was in one platoon, A Company, which only had sixteen soldiers plus one cook. We were in the compound that made Cortina GT wiring systems. We had two men out on prowler patrol, and this compound was ringed by a fence. It was quite a large area, and over to one side was an RMP detachment with Land Rovers. We all lived in huts made of aluminium. This was the way of building temporary accommodation in those days for the military. Anyway, the rest of us were lying on our beds reading when a report came over the radio that the patrol was being stoned by a group of youths outside the wire.

I don't know to this day how it started. Whether the youths had been abusive and the patrol had answered back, I don't know. Anyway, stones were thrown into the compound by these youths.,, they were soon joined by others. This was not to be a quiet Sunday.

All hell broke loose. The group of youths became a crowd, and the crowd turned into hundreds. An all-out attack took place against the compound. They were ripping the fence down where we stood. We had tin shields and batons, we fired rubber bullets, which at that time were hopeless, and we had to have permission to fire gas. What we didn't know was the road below us, called Loan More Road, was being barricaded, and we were trapped. As far as the crowd was concerned, they were going to rip us apart. It was obvious we were in trouble, deep trouble. They had laid a new road over the existing one with bricks and bottles and any other missiles that could be thrown. A dumper truck was loaded up with gas bottles, big orange ones, and set on fire, then sent down the hill into the compound. A JCB was driven straight down the hill to break through the compound. Unfortunately for the driver, who tried to jump out of the JCB, it overturned on top of him, and it was obvious the crowd was not going to lift a JCB without mechanical help, which they didn't have.

It was clear this situation was extremely serious. The platoon commander, who was a colour sergeant named Sid, was unflappable. I had never seen him draw his baton in all the battles we had been in. He was also carrying a Browning 9 mm pistol. Not only did he have the baton in his hand, he had the pistol out as well. I knew he was worried, very worried.

We were ordered two at a time to go to our accommodations and get the 7.62 SLRs. This was now a serious situation. It was obvious batons and shields weren't working. They were in the compound. They were on us. This was like Rorke's Drift. . We put away our batons and loaded our rifles and fixed our bayonets. If they came any closer, they would meet with the consequences. And this we were about to do, should the command be given.

There were thousands and thousands of rioters, all throwing bricks, bottles, and paving slabs, anything they could get hold of to kill us. This brought back memories of the Bogside, we were in the same situation again.

At this stage I didn't know if anyone knew what was going on. We hadn't seen the RMPs, who were hiding in their huts, obviously behind their pistols and SMGs. We didn't have that luxury, as we were on the sharp end. This was serious. It went on all night and into the next day. We held our ground. The following day came, and what we didn't know was that military units from all over Northern Ireland were being assembled for a rescue mission. It couldn't come soon enough. I know how they felt at Rorke's Drift in Africa. I was at the Battle of Bligh's Lane.

And then, just as we thought all was lost and that we would have to use our weapons, a column of armoured pigs, all battened down—this means all the hatches were closed so nothing could get inside—ran the barricade on Loan More Road, smashing through it and up the hill through the crowd into the compound. The rioters couldn't get hold of the vehicles. these vehicles were going too fast, and all the rioters could do was get out of the way. These vehicles also had chains that dragged along the road just beneath them. There was a switch in the cabin that could be turned on to electrify the outside of the vehicle so no one could climb on it.

These vehicles were driving onto the compound. They all turned and formed in a line. The back doors were opened, and out of the front of one of the vehicles appeared a colour sergeant from the Royal Artillery, while out of the backs of the vehicles cases of gas, CS gas, were unloaded. I remember the colour sergeant saying to me, 'That is the advantage of being in the artillery: you can direct fire.' He then called for everyone who had a baton gun to join him. I had a baton gun but no ammunition—that was long since used. There must have been about ten of us, including the artillery members he brought with him.

The artillery soldiers were running round with cases of ammunition, opening them at our feet and exposing the cartridges inside. He gave the order to load and directed that we fired all at once to the right-hand side of the hill, where the crowd was. We all fired at once, ten rounds of gas landing among them. They ran. He then said to reload and directed us to the left-hand side of the hill. The command 'fire' was given, and we all fired ten rounds, which landed to the left-hand side, so that the crowd ran from the right and over to the left to get away from the gas. At the same time two scout helicopters were circling above, dropping CS gas grenades into the crowd. This was not their day. I looked to my right and saw what must have been at least one company of a Scottish regiment proceeding up the hill with Maxi shields in front of them. The shields were six feet high and made of Perspex. They were shoulder to shoulder across the road, pushing the crowd back.

On the left came a company of Royal Green Jackets doing exactly the same move on the crowd, back up the hill. As I looked to the right I saw one of the Scottish soldiers get hit in the face with a brick, and what happened next was completely amazing to me. It was like being on the battlefield at one of the famous battles between the Scottish and English armies back in the day. He threw his helmet to the floor, threw his baton and shield down, ripped off his flak jacket, and ran into the crowd like a possessed man. He had bright ginger hair, and I thought, *There's a fiery Jock. God help the Paddies.* And at that point, without a spoken word, the whole company of Scottish soldiers threw down their shields, helmets, batons, and flak jackets and were off, attacking the crowd in support of their comrade. It was carnage. Never had this been seen before. The officers were running around like headless chickens trying to control their men, who were completely frothing at the mouth with anger and aggression. The crowd, thousands of them, were running. They had never seen this before and didn't want to be on the end of it. They were brave, but not as brave as the Scottish infantry company.

The Jocks ran at the Paddies, the Jocks were fighting an uphill battle, the Paddies were trying to run, but the Jocks were on them. There was no escape. While this was going on we were firing gas, lots of gas, to disperse the crowd, but I think they ran mainly because of the Jocks. Well done, that Scottish Infantry company, we all thought.

That night we were pinned down by constant machine-gun fire from Thompson submachine guns, pistols, rifles, RPG sevens, nail bombs, blast bombs, and petrol bombs. They tried hard to kill us all. My platoon was moved out the next day. We had survived the battle of Bligh's Lane, having stood our ground—only sixteen of us and a cook. Yes, he was there with his rifle in the front line with the rest of us. We needed every man we had.

There should have been a medal for Sid, the commander, and the rest of us should have at least got MIDs, including the cook. We were brave, and if you've ever been in a situation like that, you know what I mean. And remember, the majority of us were under twenty. I think there might have been only three people older than that.

Sadly, Sid and Rev have gone to the spirit world in recent years. They were two of the defenders at the battle of Bligh's Lane.

This tour of duty went on for two years. We had everything thrown at us in this time: nail bombs, blast bombs, and petrol bombs, rocket-propelled grenades and homemade explosives, and bullets from pistols, rifles, and machine guns. Yes, it was clear they didn't like us and didn't want us there. Having said this, I found that generally the people of Northern Ireland were the most hospitable people I've ever met. Not everyone was involved in violence. Many had to live with it; it wasn't a choice.

The life of the soldier in Northern Ireland was very hard in those days—very little sleep, insufficient manpower, and very poor equipment, for the British Army was in the dark ages at this time. Defence equipment was not a priority. However, we were still expected to do the job, and of course the British squaddie always has done his job, regardless of the situation, and always will; that's the nature of the beast. We never gave aggression, but only met it head-on. For an army with no experience of this type of situation, I feel we did extremely well. It is very easy to judge through history when you were not there on the sharp end, taking it blow for blow as we did. And remember, the average age was between seventeen and a half and twenty—just kids out of school. What life had we seen?

Bob at seventeen years old in Northern Ireland at Ebrington Barracks, 1970. This photograph shows Bob standing by a water cannon used to control riots in the city of Londonderry (Derry). It was not intended to harm anyone, but to just soak them, pushing them back from what they were doing and discouraging them from further illegal action.

Here you see Bob standing by a Mark 2 Ferret Scout car. This vehicle had a .30 calibre Browning machine gun fixed into the turret. Bob never saw the gun used in all of his two years of this tour of duty. This vehicle belonged to the recce platoon, which Bob would become a member of in later years in Cyprus. He would also learn to drive in one of these Ferret Scout cars. Isn't it amazing, what our country expected of young men like the one in this photo, just out of school? Do you think it was too much? I know that at this age people were fighting in the First and Second World Wars.

Bob is seen here and is the subject of a newspaper report regarding rioting in Northern Ireland. As you can see, Bob is in the thick of it, standing in the foreground here with his shield and baton, protecting the other soldiers behind him who have just made an arrest and are being attacked by a very large mob of rioters.

Once again, in this picture Bob has only just turned eighteen years old. He is up against grown men twice his age, but, as always, the British soldier stands firm in the face of adversity.

6

POSTED TO CYPRUS

As a reward for all our hard work, we were posted for two years to Cyprus, a fun seaside island, or so we thought until we got there and had a new commanding officer, Lieutenant Colonel D. C. Thorn, the most professional solider you could ever meet. His aim was to have the best battalion in the British Army, and he did.

What a CO he was. There was no let-up. It was constant work, work, work. He certainly had the material to work with, as we were fairly young, fit, and battle-weary. We had been there, seen it, and done it, and he built on that strength. We were in a new theatre, open areas—an almost desert environment, hot in the day and cold at night. Once again, next to no equipment, but what we did have was in good condition.

I was still in A Company, as I had been in Northern Ireland. Still a private, I didn't feel I was getting anywhere. We would just spend days walking across training areas, building sangars from rock that we found. It was getting boring. I decided I needed more of the army; I needed a bigger challenge. I'd noticed that the recce platoon had vehicles, Land Rovers stripped down to their basic bodies—no roofs, no windscreens, only the basic vehicles—and also the Ferret armoured car. This was for me. This platoon were looked up to by the rest of the battalion. If you were in the recce platoon, you were a top soldier. I applied and got the job

I had completed signals training, B1 and B2, whilst in A Company. This meant that I was a good signaller. I could also do Morse code. All of this was a requirement of the recce platoon and had helped me get the job. However, we were still short on equipment, as usual. We had heavy machine guns, GPMGs, but no mounts, so we couldn't mount the guns in the vehicles and instead had to sit them on sandbags, which was very unprofessional. I wasn't happy with this, so we went to the MT to speak to the REME and asked if they could make gun mounts. I was told that it would have to be approved and that it would not be easy. We were devastated, as we needed them. They never came. When we were posted from Cyprus to Tidworth to take on the Arctic warfare roll all the vehicles, that we were issued with had gun mounts exactly like we wanted, so we knew they were already in existence—all they would have had to do was order them, but no, we'd had to go without.

We trained and trained and trained.. We spent all our time either on the training area or on the ranges. We were always out there. As a battalion we took part in every military competition that there was on the island, and most of the time we won. No one could touch us. We had the fitness, the team spirit, and most importantly, Lieutenant Colonel D. C. Thorn at the helm. What more could we ask for?

Cyprus is a lovely island. Surely many of you have been on holiday there. Since leaving the army, I have been back to the holiday town of Paphos twice, in 2006 and 2009. They say that once you've visited you will return, and this is true. They have famous monuments like Aphrodite's Rock. It's all there. Unfortunately, the Turkish laid siege to half the island in 1974 and is still divided to this day. My battalion had only left to go back to England three months before the invasion of 1974. There was no sign that it was coming, but we would have been ready—we always were.

It was a lovely posting, especially for families, what with the beaches, the all-year-round sun, plenty of places to visit, and lots of tourist spots. In the forces you can do any sport you want in Cyprus. You name it, they got it, and you can become quite proficient at it. That's a good thing about the army: if you're good at a sport, they encourage you to carry on. And I was always good at athletics: cross-country running, field sports, and I played rugby for my school, the depot, the Royal Anglian Regiment, and the First Battalion. I just seemed to have a flair for it, and later on I would play squadron rugby in 22 SAS. As I said before also, we did a lot of training in Cyprus, and shooting was one of the main things I made to battalion team. Later on I would go on to become a sniper. All this had started from owning an air rifle as a boy, so it wasn't a misspent youth.

I was sent on an NCOs cadre. This was for ranks from private to lance corporal. I did well. I remember coming eighth on the course with a C+ grade—just missed a B and don't know why. (The problem with military courses is if you upset one of the instructors in any way, it will affect your grade. Something must have gone wrong somewhere. Having said that, C+ is not bad.) On completion of the course, I was promoted straightaway. This didn't go down well with the others in the platoon, as some of them had been there longer than me, The problem was they had a quota of privates, lance corporals, and corporals, along with just one sergeant, one colour sergeant, and the captain, who is platoon commander. I soon learnt that the recce platoon at the time was a dead man's shoes. You could serve out the rest of your army career there and you wouldn't get promoted, so a move was the only answer, as I had been there two years and this was enough.

7

KENYA

The battalion was sent on exercise to Kenya while still in Cyprus. This was to train in secondary jungle and bush areas. The recce platoon's job was to go in advance of the battalion, find the enemy, patrol out from base camps, etc.

D. C. Thorn was still in charge, so we knew what was coming. It would be no joyride. After about three weeks' training we had two days off, and after a local night out it was planned to go to a game reserve. The idea was to take photos of big wild animals in their natural habitat. We had two Land Rovers. Most of the party got on the front Land Rover. I tried to, but it was full. What I did not know and was later to find out was that Spirit was looking after me, again.

I got in the back vehicle with the two Charlies: Charlie Shropshire and Charlie Shirley. We set off. The roads in Kenya are not the best, it must be said, and if you think we have a problem with potholes, you'll love Kenya.

All was well—a bit fast for the roads, but it was a straight run. The front Land Rover had the canvas top rolled back so they could stand up and view the animals when we got to the reserve. This would prove to be a lifesaver.

We had been going for some time when the road forked left, right, and straight on. In the middle of the fork, set back from the road, was a signboard that said 'Bata' and pointed to the left, giving directions to the game reserve.

The driver of the front vehicle saw it at the last minute, and instead of slowing down and passing the sign, he tried to turn left. He was going too fast to make the turn.

Then the unthinkable happened: the front Land Rover went straight through the Bata sign, to our horror, and what happened next was a complete nightmare. It was like a Hollywood film set. On the other side of the sign there was a big drop of at least two meters into a field. The Land Rover took off into the air, came down on its front bumper, and turned upside down.

It had no roll cage. One man jumped out of the back, Paul Smith, an ex-para who had left the army after an injury to work as a paramedic, then rejoined in our unit. He survived but had injuries. The scene was disastrous: bodies everywhere, screams, a massive dust cloud, all of the casualties covered in thick dust and dirt, the Land Rover's wheels still spinning around. The platoon colour sergeant, Roy Smith, was on the floor with his ear hanging on a thread of skin and covered in dust and dirt. As I got to him he raised his arm for me to help him. What could I do? He needed more than first aid. This was a major incident. We needed a top trauma team, and fast.

The rolling back of the canvas on the Land Rover saved lives. If this had not been done, no one would have been thrown out, and everyone would have been crushed. Two people passed to the spirit world that day, Bill Owings and Eddy Edwards, both good men.

We were in the middle of nowhere. We had a HF radio in the second vehicle, which we managed to get help on, and we were joined by a convoy of nuns in VW minibuses, who were a great help. Not the best day of my army career.

I know that Spirit was with me that day and had been from the start of my life. I did not know then, but I do now. Thank you, Spirit.

8

POSTED TO TIDWORTH, HAMPSHIRE

After our hard two years in Cyprus, we were posted to Tidworth, Hampshire. What a posting. We were the AMFL Battalion. This stands for Ace Mobile Force Land. We were responsible for NATO's northern flank, Norway.

Unless someone moved, you couldn't get promoted in the recce platoon, and so as long as I stayed there, I would not get a second stripe. I decided to move not back to A Company but to B Company. I don't know, looking back, if this was the right choice. There is a saying, 'Better the devil you know'; however, there is also another saying, 'Don't go back.' So I didn't. I moved on. Unfortunately, it probably wasn't the best move, as posting in an NCO stopped someone else from getting promoted from a private soldier, because I'd moved in over him and got the job. A lance corporal is second-in-command of his section; this meant I was responsible for the GPMG machine gun, the section's main firepower. A private soldier and I would work the gun and carry the ammunition, plus our own weapons.

I kept asking the platoon sergeant to put me on a corporals cadre so I could get promoted. He didn't do this right away, as it takes a year to get on one. Eventually it came. We all turned up on day one of the course with thirty others. We were given a squad instructor, and as usual I got the short straw—the laziest sergeant you ever met, biding his time in the training wing as no one wanted him in any of the companies. I tried hard and I worked hard but got a bad report. This wasn't good, as I needed promotion to move on and climb the ladder. I wanted to get into the sergeants' mess. Once you got three stripes in the battalion, people looked up to you; you could get good jobs and lots of courses. I liked courses to learn as much as I could and to get as high up as I could on completion of the cadre, and some weeks later I had to go in front of my OC to get my report. At this stage I hadn't a clue what it contained.

I was called into the OC's office for my course report. My OC was called Major Gilbert Connor—a really nice man who had been a troop or squadron commander in the SAS. This commanded great respect from me. You could talk to this man. He was human. He knew how to handle men. I marched in, halted, and saluted. He had my report in front of him. I stood there at attention in front of him. He said, 'At ease.' This meant you weren't bolt upright but stood at a relaxed position. He said, 'I've got your report here from the corporals cadre,' and he used his favourite saying: 'You see, you can't hold a good man down, and I'm sending you to Brecon. The para battle school has just changed to the all-arms course. You will go there and you will show them.' It was clear the report wasn't good. I saluted and left the office.

I went to Brecon, and along with me came Chico Duncan, a good mate, a lance corporal as well. We worked hard. We knew our stuff. We stood out. We were in a classroom. I was sat next to a lad called Alan, in the Black Watch. He said to me, 'If you were in my battalion and you knew what you know, you would be a sergeant.' I thanked him, remembering what the major had told me: 'It's hard to hold a good man down.' The course was physically demanding,. I didn't expect an easy ride, nor did I get one. I completed the course, which was six weeks of physical and mental stress: constantly being tested, day and night, across the training areas of Sennybridge—navigating, setting ambushes. We all had to be the platoon sergeant and also the platoon commander. We were under pressure always. I did well. and I felt pleased with myself.

On return to Tidworth, back to B Company, I had only been back a couple of days when the company sergeant major said to me, 'Corporal Curry, I've got your Brecon report here. You did well. You got a C+. Well done. You will be on Company Commanders interview today.' Unfortunately, while I was away the company commanders had changed, and we had been given the laziest, most flamboyant officer the battalion had ever known—well, certainly the worst I've ever met. I did not like this man. He didn't have a good word for anyone. Looking back, I don't think I had an interview with him. I went straight on to the CO, the commanding officer, once again a very good officer—nice man, he was, human, and talked to men properly. We lined up outside the CO's office. The RSM was there, shouting at everyone as usual. Well, that was his job. He didn't have much else to do.

I was marched into the CO's office. He sat at his desk and behind him stood the adjutant. The CO said, 'Well done, Corporal Curry. Excellent report. If you keep this up, you will be getting promoted.' At this point the adjutant said, 'We are promoting him to corporal.'

'Oh,' said the CO. 'Well, well done.' And that was it. I was marched out holding two stripes. I was now a full corporal. Full corporals were held in high esteem in the battalion. You didn't get there unless you were qualified.

As we could only practice at warfare in the Arctic, we spent most of our time on Salisbury Plain sitting in trenches, not dug out of the ground but comprised of white tape laid out on the grass in the shape of trenches. Then we would do helicopter drills—not in real ones, but we had chairs laid out to represent the insides of a helicopter. We would get onto the helicopter and get off the helicopter. Packs on, packs off. All day. We even had a volunteer to play the pilot. He was one of the platoon, who had to sit in the front row of seats like a real pilot.

We went to Norway every January for six weeks—four weeks spent down south practicing skills in the snow and two weeks up north on exercise Arctic Express, where we were joined with the marines and other units. This exercise was like it was on the Russian front during World War II. I don't know how they survived. The average day would be -42°C. 'Cold' is not the word. Everything was frozen. Anything metal froze. Cloth froze. Eyebrows. The hair up your nose. It was hard work trying to motivate ten men when you were fed up yourself. It wasn't just the work, it was the organisation, or lack of it. And no one seemed to have a clue what we were doing. Someone would come up with an idea about what to do today and we would do it. Our equipment was poor. We had leather boots that got soaked straightaway, not waterproof, so they didn't work. It was a sorry place.

The OC was a very lazy person. He did not like work, and every opportunity he could, he got off it, with a fake injury or something. I had no respect for him. He was one of those flamboyant types, not a real solider.

I was getting fed up with all of this. Every January we would be shipped off to Norway for another six weeks in the snow and the disorganisation that went with it. We had a motto, 'Hurry up and wait.'

It was on one of these Norway tours that my life would change.

I was standing at a road checkpoint with my section of men when a tall man wearing a white cam kit came up to me and said, 'You Bob Curry?' I replied yes. He said, 'I'm Geordie, and I'm with you for a week.'

I replied, 'Fine. Where are you from? What unit?' He said, 'SAS.' Well, I had only heard of the SAS. I had never met one. Geordie spent a very memorable week with my section, and at the end I knew what I had to do: selection for the SAS. I could do it, as I was ready. I was very fit, and my determination would get me through, as well as my excellent military training that I'd received so far, mostly from junior soldiers.

9

SAS SELECTION

Before I could go on SAS selection, I had to apply for it. This meant going in front of the OC, the one I got on with so well. He was his normal negative self. He said, 'You won't pass that. The fittest man I have ever known couldn't pass. What chance have you got?' I looked at him and said to myself, *How can you say that?* I was one of the fittest section commanders in the battalion, and my section had come second place in the battalion section competition, out of at least sixty sections. I'd proved myself.

I also had to see the second-in-command of the battalion to go on selection for the SAS. He put it pretty bluntly to me: 'You'd better pass. Otherwise, your career here will stop.' Wonderful—such support. You weren't allowed to better yourself. I really felt that they were envious. They knew they couldn't do it, so they didn't want anyone else to. And they were bothered by the thought that there was someone in their ranks who could possibly achieve the practically unachievable, as it was looked upon by many soldiers, then and now.

By now my life was being guided by Spirit, as it had been when Geordie had been sent to me. He was the messenger. This was my life's course, my direction. I was being told to do this: *This is your future.* I had to learn the lessons of the past to drive me on to achieve better things, and I did. Thank you, Spirit.

I managed to work my way through all the obstacles that were thrown at me, filled out the paperwork, and went on an interview with the CO, who was a much better, laid-back person, with the rank of lieutenant colonel. He was doing well in the army and liked others to achieve, so I was encouraged by him. At last, this was good. I finally had someone's blessing.

Finally I arrived at the SAS Camp Bradbury lines in Hereford. As it was then all wooden huts, it reminded me of the days when I was a junior soldier in the same type of camp. No money had been spent on the camp for years. The camp was guarded by the Ministry of Defence police who were armed. This was unusual at the time because many military camp guards only had lumps of wood to walk about with. You could see that life was more serious here, and the threat level was higher than in the battalion where I had come from. I was allocated a bed space in the training wing. My room there accommodated about twenty others, most of them from the paras and marines, and only a handful of us from other units.

It was obvious from the start that the paras saw themselves as above the rest of us, as we didn't jump out of planes. Therefore we were all 'crap hats.' That is the airborne forces' way of describing people who are not parachute trained. However, this didn't matter to me, as I knew that even though I didn't jump out of planes, I was as good and qualified as any other man on the course, and this would become apparent as time went on.

The course started with a talk from the CO of the 22 SAS. We were all in one room. He introduced himself by his first name and surname. This was totally out of character for officers in the army in those days. It was our first sign that we were to be treated like men and that we now had the opportunity to join the big boys' club.

'I'll take on every one of you if you can pass this selection course,' he said. There were 180 men in that room. There were paras, marines, and just about every unit in the British Armed Forces, and everyone was looking at everyone else thinking the same thing: *Look at the size of him. What chance have I got?* I was to find out later that size doesn't matter in this case. It's ability you need.

After his speech we were taken to the stores to draw equipment required for the course. This included Bergens, which are backpacks that we had to carry. This annoyed the paras and marines, as they had their airborne forces Bergens that they had trained with and padded out in the right places just to be told that they couldn't use them now. We were all told to load our Bergens with thirty-five pounds of kit and then go to the armoury to draw an FN rifle and get on the four-tonne trucks at the guard room. We were off to the Brecon Beacons for our first test, the Fan Dance.

We all arrived at the Storey Arms side of the Brecon Beacons to be told, 'Everyone off the trucks. Bergens on. Follow me.' One of the badged training staff ran off up the mountain. We all had to follow like sheep, but this was a race. We had to run to the top of Pen y Fan to the trig point, down the other side, which was very steep, called Jacob's Ladder, and then along a track called the Roman Road, until we reached the far end, passing a forestry block on our left, and finally arrived at a disused railway station joining the main road.

There was a Land Rover parked at the end by the road. The instructor who was running with us said, 'Right. Lunch break.' Not to be fooled, I had been warned about tricks that might be pulled on us, so I had a big drink of water and stuck a whole Mars bar in my mouth sideways. I did not take my pack off. I trusted no one, and I was right.

Two minutes later a new instructor jumped out of the back of the Land Rover, which was covered in a tarpaulin, and said, 'Lunch over. Follow me.' I was ready for this but many were not. There were cookers and mess tins everywhere. Off we went back along the Roman Road and up that hill again, climbing Jacob's Ladder. This is a hard task, as it is almost vertical. We were now spreading out a long way, and I was near the front somewhere.

As we started to climb back up to Pen y Fan and to the trig point, the weather got bad, very bad. It started to rain hard. It was amazing how sudden the weather came in on us. You can see how people get caught out on the hills unprepared. You must have the right equipment to be caught in this situation; without it, this could be the last thing you ever do. I stopped and put my foul-weather gear on. This was Spirit telling me what was to come, and it did. I was an experienced soldier. I knew about hypothermia and what rain and wind could do to the body by reducing the core temperature rapidly, leading to unconsciousness and then death.

As I got to the top, I was now on my own. The mist was down to whiteout conditions. I could not believe how hard the wind was blowing. It was gale-force. It came from nowhere. To test the wind's strength, I tried to fall over into it and could not; it held me up. This was incredible—the worst conditions I've ever been out in, and the problem was I was on my own. But this was what I was training for, to work as an individual, to achieve the mission regardless. This was a test to find the type of person that could achieve this without giving up, without being stopped by the weather and other obstacles thrown in his way.

It was my very good soldiering ability that got me back down that mountain that day: knowing what to do and when to do it, my outstanding navigation abilities all achieved from the army service, and of course the will to win.

On the way down the mountain I met a school party going up wearing only shorts and tee shirts. I stopped and told the teacher with them to turn back. I said it was horrendous up there and that they wouldn't make it back down in one piece. I don't think he believed me.

Finally I reached the bottom of the mountain, where the trucks were waiting for us. There were also staff members with a Land Rover, where we had to check in. I asked how long we'd had for the exercise as I knew everything was timed. I was told three hours; I'd made it well within the time.

We were told to get into our dry kit, get a brew on, and wait for the truck to fill up before we could go back to camp. There were several trucks parked, and I went to the one with the least amount of people on it. Everyone looked extremely tired and worn out. It was obvious the mountain had taken its toll on many of them. Some had climbed in their sleeping bags and were fast asleep, totally exhausted.

I got changed and put a brew on. This was achieved by means of a Hexham cooker and a metal mug placed on the top of the small, outward-opening cooker that is issued to the forces. Hexamine when lit smells very toxic. You can't use it in confined spaces, just in the open. You put a small flat block on it, like a fire lighter, and break it up and light it. It only takes a few minutes to boil a mug of water, which is then mixed with tea powder, as it has milk powder already in it. It tastes fantastic. Well, we waited and waited for everyone else to arrive. The four-tonne lorries were almost full, but we still stayed there. It was apparent that there was a problem: someone was missing.

One man had not checked in. We were told that we would all have to go and look for him. We were told to start getting changed again, back into our wet clothes and boots. We were going to have to go back up that mountain and look for the lost person. Knowing what I had just come through, I thought to myself, How? I had only just got down myself. How were we going to find someone who might not even be on the track? He could have rolled downhill in the mist and gone. But off we went back up the hill. The search was on. I wasn't looking forward to going back into that weather again, but we did. We got to the top, looking everywhere, and then the word came through: *We've found him. He's dead.*

The weather had claimed him. He was found at the top of Pen y Fan, right near the trig point. He was lying on the ground with one arm out of his Bergen strap, and he was not wearing his foul-weather gear. He had clearly attempted to remove the Bergen to put it on, but the weather had claimed him first. I had always been told in my early days in the army that as soon as it looks like rain, put your foul-weather gear on. There's no point in putting it on when you're already wet; the damage is done. It was clear that he had not known this. Otherwise, he would have done it long before and maybe still been with us today, and not gone to the spirit world early.

It was a long, quiet drive back. One of the DS training staff sat in the back of the four-tonne truck with us and was asked by someone, 'What happens now, staff?' to the reply, 'Well, he's failed, hasn't he?' They were only looking for the best, and that was now obvious.

The year was 1979. August. The day Ted Heath's boat, Morning Cloud, had the problem in the fast net boat race. What a day, and what unbelievable weather—the worst I've ever seen. As I said before, I leaned into the wind with my Bergen on and my rifle and belt kit and tried to fall over, but the wind held me up. It just shows how fast conditions can change in the mountains of our beloved country.

I went on from test to test. The course was designed to weed out the weak individuals who would give up on a daily basis, or go sick to the medical officer and get RTU through injury to save face back at their units. The truth was they didn't have what it took. Nothing was going to stop me. I had so much drive and determination, regardless of what they threw at me, and I saw much bigger and stronger men than me fall by the wayside with the words, 'I can't go on.' But not me. I could. My OC in the battalion was wrong. I had what it took to get into the best and toughest unit in any military force in the world, the British SAS.

We spent three weeks charging around the mountains with physical tests every day. They were designed to make us give up, admit that we couldn't handle it, that it was too tough for us. Not for me. This would never happen. On the fourth week, known as 'test week,' we were up every day at 0430 hours and out of the gate on the trucks. This is what all the training was about: Could we pass the final physical week? Every day the distances got farther and the weight got heavier, and all against the clock.

And then, finally, it was the final test. We were out at 0430 hours as usual that day, and then, returning to camp after a long march, we went out again on the ground at 2359 hours. When the final test get underway, we had fifty-six kilometres to march in twenty hours. I must've been carrying one hundred pounds, including an FN rifle and belt kit, which would be around thirty pounds, and the Bergen, which was probably seventy pounds. Off we went like on a mad race.

It was dark and we had to navigate across the mountains. Follow no one, trust no one. You were on your own. If they had it wrong, then so had you, so you had to be on your own.

We went on through the night and the next day, into the afternoon. Yes, I was tired, but determined. This was not going to beat me. This was my final chance to win the coveted winged dagger that I'd always wanted to have—something that mattered. I remember the final two hundred yards of the march, which were across the reservoir bridge. And there stood at the end the OC of the training wing, smiling at me because I'd made it. I was a contender for the regiment. My time was sixteen and a half hours and A-grade.

10

CONTINUATION TRAINING

Monday morning and we were on parade. There were now only fifty-six of us left after the first four weeks. They had weeded out the weak limbs, the Walter Mittys. The cowboys were all gone. Only the strong and the determined had survived. We were now going to do ten days' training. This involved foreign weapons, patrolling techniques, and a lot of the skills that we would need to serve in the regiment alongside the other badged personnel.

We would go to a military training area on a daily basis and be put through tactics training, including patrolling and specialising in four-man ops, helicopter deployments, and foreign weapons. We had to know how to strip and assemble an AK-47 in case we were in a situation where we needed to use one. We fired these weapons on the ranges along with many other weapons from various countries around the world. We had to be good with them; one day lives might depend on it.

The physical side didn't stop. We still did runs every day, and they were trying to get people to throw their hands in. It was like the staff were competing to see who could get rid of the most people. They only wanted the ones who deserved to be there.

I got a knee injury, which wasn't good, but I kept going. They knew about it, and I was sent to the physiotherapist for brief treatment, but I still did all the other work that the rest of the course did. This injury would haunt me. The next phase of our training and the most intensive was the jungle. But when you have an injury like I had, you have to carry on, because if you were behind enemy lines and you were injured, you would still have to achieve your aim. This was what it was all about, the stamina and determination of the individual. You had to have what it took to be part of this fighting unit.

We did many things, including making up belt kits. These were what you wore around your waist, consisting of water bottles and carriers, emergency rations, survival equipment, and pouches with ammunition to defend yourself against aggressors. I always carried as much ammunition as I could. We were issued four magazines for our AR-15s; however, I always had ten, as there was no way I was going to run out of ammunition in a critical situation. The worst sound a soldier can hear in a firefight is 'click'—this means no ammo.

We had to have medical supplies and were issued with morphine in case we were shot or badly injured. We wore it around our necks so it could be self-administered. It was contained in ampoules, which you would remove and inject into your thigh. We were given extensive medical training: we could insert a drip, give an injection, stop bleeding by tourniquet, and achieve everything needed for instant help for a wounded patient or ourselves. And we always had a compass attached to us, plus a map of the local area. Map reading by now was second nature; we could do it almost in our sleep. We wouldn't get lost—no chance. And we would practice day and night to find our way.

We attended many lectures explaining how things were now done—i.e., not the way the battalion did it. This was different. We were down to four men, who were not a fighting force to take on large enemy units; we were there for reconnaissance, destruction, working with partisans anywhere we were in the world.

We had to have the ability to work with the locals, the ones on our side, and defeat the aggressor wherever it may be. That is one of the things that the regiment is good at: working in small groups and training in foreign countries to teach the locals to help themselves against the invaders, people who want to take their homes and their land and sometimes their lives.

But they had to trust us, so we had to contact them and be the masters of hearts and minds so they would be on our side—because if we were betrayed to a large force, it could be the end for us. However, we had the ability. If called upon to fight, fight we would, with the aggression of a trapped tiger. SAS does not only stand for the Special Air Service Regiment. It also stands for Speed, Aggression, Surprise—and most of all, maximum violence.

And this would be seen at the Iranian Embassy in London on May 5, 1980. This is what happens when you release the tiger.

We flew back to England, loaded up the transport with equipment and all the Bergens, and travelled back to Hereford. We put our Bergens on our beds in the bashers and handed in all the stores and weapons. We were told to be in the blue room at 1500 hours. We all knew what was coming next—to some the end of the road. It would be all over. Chop time.

11

THE JUNGLE

On completion of this training we prepared to go to the jungle for weeks of training and tests. It was common knowledge that this was the make or break of everyone, and on return we would all be put into a room and told who had passed and who had failed the jungle phase.

This was definitely the toughest test that we would be put through, and we knew that if we won we would get into the semifinals of this course. There was no better place to test the skills and determination of a soldier than in a jungle environment. It's all in there: creepy crawlies like snakes, spiders, and hornets, the fact that every tree has got spikes on it, and the fact that everything that crawls will bite you or suck your blood. The undergrowth dies all the time, and fresh roots grow through. It's such a hard, tough environment.

You train with heavy weights, navigating through the undergrowth and over mountains with minimal food, heavy radios, and lots of ammunition and explosives. You have to get from A to B in set times. You have to plan

ambushes, fighting in rivers and mud. You have to cut helipads and blow
them. You receive extensive explosives training. You're given written and
verbal tests—sat out in the rain and asked, *What is this? What is that? How
do you do this? How do you do that? Show me your weapon. It's rusty. Keep
it clean. It will save your life one day.* You know you can't keep it clean; it's
in the mud or it's in the river, in the undergrowth, as you are constantly
battling. The good thing about the jungle is that nothing moves at night,
so you are guaranteed to get some good hammock time, but only after
you've covered your tracks and made sure that you have not attracted the
attention of any interested party; otherwise things could go wrong, ter-
ribly wrong. However, you prepare for this.

Off we went, kits packed, ready for the unknown, not knowing what was
coming or whether we would survive. Everyone talked about the jungle.
We had never been there before, but I knew it was full of beasties, as we
call them—things that bit you, things that stung you, things that buried
themselves in you and gave you diseases. *Well, let's give it a go. I hope it
doesn't happen to me.* We arrived and were told to sort our kits out, as we
were going in tomorrow morning, by helicopter.

As we flew over the jungle canopy, I looked down but couldn't see anything—just the canopy of trees rising up and then down. You knew by the
way the trees were that there was a lot of contours to this countryside,
which meant walking up and down hills in the mud among the trees. This
was going to be fun, I was sure.

We landed on the LP landing point. The RSM stood at the ten o'clock position of the disc. You always disembark from a helicopter at ten o'clock or
two o'clock. The pilot sits at twelve o'clock, and you never go to the rear,
as you run the risk of walking into the tail rotor, which many unfortunate souls have done. 'Follow me!' he shouted, and off he ran. We tried to

follow him, but we had all of our kits: Bergens, belt kits, weapons. There was mud everywhere—one pace forward and two paces back along a long track, slipping and sliding and trying to keep up. Eventually we got to a clearing, and he stopped. He told us to get our notebooks out and write down everything we had seen on the track on the way.

To be truthful, there was only one thing we had seen: mud, and lots of it—and, of course, the back of the man in front of us. No one had seen anything. We were failures. The RSM produced a piece of paper from his pocket. He read out a list of military items that were hidden in the jungle along the track. I think that if there had been a four-tonne lorry parked there, we would have missed it. We had only been concerned with keeping up and not being left behind, not knowing how long this track would be and how long we would be on it.

He then reached down behind him and produced a pole, and on the end of it was a snake. 'This,' he said, 'is a jumping Tommy Gough, one of the deadliest snakes in the world, and I found it in my basher area. Keep your eyes open and don't put anything on the floor, or you may get a surprise.'

Well, you can imagine how we all felt now. This snake was massive. He had put a sharpened stick through its head, and the mouth was open. Its fangs were huge. I couldn't imagine meeting the relatives of this creature whilst attempting to sleep among them. He said, 'Right. You will now be broken up into patrols.' And he read out the names of who was going with which instructor. I was assigned to one called Tony, an ex-marine who never spoke. It was as if we were constantly being watched and tested and having secret notes written about us (we were), and the thing was that at no time during the selection course were we told how we were getting on. We were asked how we thought we were getting on, and if we said 'okay,' we would be met with a laugh from the instructor.

Many demonstrations followed: how to put a hammock up, make a pole bed, pack our kit, and carry a weapon. Many tactics were practised. We had a lean-to schoolhouse built by the local labourers, where we would learn the details of our new career and then be tested and tested again and again.

It always rains in the jungle at the same time every day. It gets dark at the same time and light at the same time every morning..

Anyway, we battled on with our training. We took on every task as it arrived, constantly staying alert, weapons in the ready position at all times; if we were sitting down making a brew or food, our weapons were always within hand's reach. If they weren't, this incurred a VC—'voluntary contribution'—which was a fine to be paid to the Regimental Association Clock Tower fund for incompetence. I was lucky I never got any VCs—belt kit always on, weapon within hand's reach always, and most importantly, ready to bug out at any time if attacked.

We learnt patrol tactics by working with four-man patrols. We walked for miles on navigation exercises, carrying all our kits, and map reading had to be spot-on. Everyone had to navigate so we would all know where we were at all times, in case we were hit or bumped by the enemy. There were drills that we had to achieve and practise. Mostly we would use live ammunition; no error of judgement would be allowed, or somebody's life would be lost.

The best type of training is real, tried, and tested—and plentiful. We were constantly being tested, all the time. We were sent out in patrols on our own to do the various tasks over several days—no DS instructor with us, but we knew he was there, not far behind, looking for signs and listening to the sounds.

Local labour had been employed to construct a school house for teaching, this was constructed of bamboo and the roof was made of leaves, there were no sides and there were bamboo poles laid out in lines like seating of a football stadium but all on the same level. At the top was a blackboard where the instructor would teach us patrol tactics, the art of survival, explosives in the form of demolitions and the different types of equipment we would use to destroy buildings, radio masts, power plants, railways, bridges and roads and anything else that needed that special touch. We would go out constantly practicing these drills that were taught in the schoolhouse. There would be loud explosions and birds and wildlife would flee in great quantities, we were wrecking their environment and peace, we were not good neighbours to have!

Live firing of our personal weapons and support weapons was paramount in this training. I remember putting in an attack on a simulated position along a riverbank up to my neck in water giving covering fire with my personal weapon while others moved forward. I had been submerged in the river most of the day when my DS, Tony came up to me and said 'Show me your machete', this had to be attached to your waist belt at all times. I looked at him and at first couldn't take in what he was saying, there I was in the middle of a big fight, live rounds flying everywhere, tracer, 40mm grenades, smoke grenades, hand grenades, all going off all around us and he wanted to see my machete. I produced it and my heart dropped, it was red with rust, well it would have been as I had been in the river all day, he just looked at me and handed it back to me and said 'Put it away'. My heart sank. My immediate thought was that I had messed up but what could I have done, of course it was rusty considering where I had been all day.

Every night we would stand to, this is where each soldier has a defensive point that he goes to, to protect the camp in case of an attack. You would have seen this on American Vietnam films like 'Platoon' where they were constantly constructing defensive positions and stand to positions. It is supposed to give you cover from fire and somewhere to go if you are attacked by mortars or artillery. We were constantly wet, but we had two sets of kit, a wet set and a dry set. The dry set stayed in a plastic bag tied up in your Bergen, the wet set was for daytime use. At night after stand to you would put on your dry set and get in your pole bed or hammock. In the morning just before stand to you put on your wet set which was always fun and put your dry set back into the plastic bag and tie it up inside your Bergen. Your kit never dried in the jungle so if you kept your dry set on you would always sleep wet which some people did exactly that.

Our time in the jungle was finally over. We had lost a considerable amount of weight, and my hands were covered in mosquito bites. So was my face. Yes, we had repellent, but it didn't work against these mosquitoes—they were tough.

We were going back to England to find out our fates. Had we passed, or were we failures? All too soon to be revealed.
We had to load all the equipment onto helicopters and fly it back to the main base camp where we had initially arrived. All our kit had to be washed and checked for creepy crawlies, the royal air force didn't want any surprises on their aircraft! This was a massive task as there was a lot of equipment, all weapons had to be cleaned and oiled and placed in weapon rolls which looks like a big tool roll with sleeves, these were rolled up and strapped up. Loading the aircraft which was a VC10 seemed to take forever, everyone did their best knowing that we were still being watched. Eventually we passed through passport control and were all loaded on the plane back to England and to await our fate.

We arrived at RAF Brize Norton in Oxfordshire, our transport was waiting for us which was four tonne lorries and coaches, once again the aircraft had to be unloaded and the lorries had to be loaded with the equipment from the aircraft then we all had to pass through immigration to make sure we were who we were supposed to be and no-one had sneaked in! Eventually onto the transport and away back to Hereford. This journey was silent, we knew we were going to find out our fate, had we passed or would we be going home that day, no one knew except the DS, had all this been for nothing, had we got what it takes to become a member of the world's most elite fighting force?

Back in Hereford from the Jungle

We arrived back in Hereford. The usual chaos, unload the trucks, this was going to take a while as they were full then everyone had to sort out their personal kit from a big pile which was developing behind the trucks but we had been there before and everything was labelled so it didn't take too long, all the weapons had to go to the armoury to be handed in and then back to the huts where we had been staying before our jungle trip. We put our Bergens on our beds, there was no point in emptying them as we didn't know who was staying or who was going, in the event of going, they were packed ready. We were told to be at the blue room, this was the briefing room at the camp at1500 hours. We were walking around like condemned men. Eventually 1500 hours came.

We were all assembled in the Blue Room. We knew from others that had gone before us that this was the time the course would be finally chopped down—by this I mean we had all been watched closely during the training. The staff had had meetings to decide who they wanted and who they didn't. We were about to find out who they didn't want.

The squadron sergeant major walked into the room. His name was Lofty Wiseman, a big man from London, a tower of strength not to be messed with—however, one of the nicest men I've ever met in my life, and one I now call a true friend. The silence was eerie. You could almost hear hearts beating. This was chop time. All of your efforts could have been for nothing; you could be going back to your unit.

I couldn't imagine turning up in front of my OC a failure. I would have never lived it down, and my career would have been ended, anyway. The squadron sergeant major looked around the room as he stood at the lectern and said, 'We are starting work on Monday. Unfortunately, the following won't be with us.' I can't describe the atmosphere in that room; you had to be there. I can only equate it to a man standing on the dock awaiting his fate, and the judge putting on the black cloth on top of his wig, as it used to be when a man was condemned to death.

This is how it felt. Every man in that room was asking himself the same questions: *Is it me? Am I going back to my unit? Have I failed?* And then the names were read out, one at a time. These people were going back to their units, RTU. I was sat next to a para who had been telling me before the sergeant major came in how well he had done. I wasn't a para, so maybe my name was about to be read out. The names came. The looks on the faces—big men, paras, marines, not required, failed. What chance did I have? I was just waiting for it, like a bullet to the heart.

And then the name of the para next to me was read out. He was going home back to unit, RTU. *No*, I thought, when I heard his name. *I'm next.* The names went on. There were fifty-six of us that had returned from the jungle out of the one hundred eighty that had started the course. These numbers were now being greatly reduced. The names went on, and then sergeant major said, 'Right. See the rest of you 0830 Monday outside the training wing.'

Had I missed something? My name hadn't been called. I wasn't going back. I had passed the jungle test—unbelievable. I cannot describe how I felt. I'd got through the second-biggest test I was going to have thrown at me on this course, and I had survived.

We had the weekend off. All I can say is a few pints of beer were drunk that weekend. It was a small band of happy members of that selection course that were left; however, we all knew we hadn't finished, and that there would be more tests, many more, before we got our winged dagger that we all wanted so very badly.

The ability to train in different parts of the world will always be a skill that special forces must be at the peak of. Here you see Bob out in the jungle on a 'hearts and minds' mission whilst in operational conditions, accepting hospitality from the locals in the form of a straw hut for the night, and pleasing the locals with gifts of boiled sweets, chocolate, batteries for their radios, and of course the compulsory game of football with the children—however, still alert to their environment. 'Hearts and minds' is an important part of warfare: win the people and they will turn their backs on the aggressors

Here Bob is sitting on an LP (landing point) waiting for a helicopter. Bob and the troop have just cut this LP out of the jungle. This task involves moving big trees—not something that can be done with a machete. Therefore explosives had to be used. This is something the SAS specialise in, making quick LPs for resupply or extraction of casualties or men. Notice Bob is holding an AR-15 rifle, this is a favourite weapon of the regiment in jungle situations, as it has full automatic fire capability and the ammunition, being 5.56 calibre, is very light to carry; therefore each soldier can have more of it

This is a view from the LP after it was cut. You can see in the distance the density of the jungle that we were working in. Jungle operations have long been one of the many skills of an SAS soldier, back to the days of Malaya and Borneo, when the regiment proved itself many times against the insurgents and without doubt the SAS became a force to be reckoned with. To this day their skills are honed in this theatre of warfare

Here we have an A-frame pole bed and shelter sheet, typical base camp accommodation built by the SAS soldier for his own comfort. Note that in this picture, which is of one of Bob's own creations, he has included a table and bench to give it some form of civilisation. However, if the soldier were moving through the jungle operationally, then he would use a hammock and shelter sheet, leaving no sign of ever being there. Two different ways of operating.

12

THE COMBAT
SURVIVAL COURSE

M onday came. We were now down to approximately twenty-three men, and we were about to start the combat survival course. This was a course for army combat survival instructors: how to live off the land, how to evade capture, and, if unfortunate enough, how to be captured and resist interrogation. This course would have greatly helped Andy McNabb when he was captured in Iraq. I know Andy. He was in the same squadron as me. We went through the same training.

There we all were, on parade. What a motley-looking crew we were. Our hair was getting really long. So were our sideboards, and most people had Mexican moustaches that went right down to the bottoms of their chins. We were joined by quite a few others who were not on the selection course. This included RAF pilots, navy pilots, helicopter crews, and various other individuals who might well find themselves in a survival situation.

The first week we were shown films on survival and lectured by individual experts, male and female, with regard to what we could eat on the land. This included terrains like hedgerows, farmers' fields, woodland, and anywhere else with the possibility of a meal that could be foraged. We also looked at making improvised shelters and starting fires without fire-lighting material. We had to learn a system where you use a bow and a block of wood; with these you create friction that will set tinder alight—not an easy task.

We were also shown what fungi we could eat. The training-wing sergeant major, Lofty Wiseman, was a renowned world expert on survival. I'm sure you've heard of him. He has written many books and starred in DVDs. He explained to us that in a survival situation you can eat anything you want, but some things will kill you.

Wise words indeed. I always went with those thoughts in mind. If I didn't like the look of it, I wouldn't eat it, and would never eat it raw—always cooked, if possible. It makes me laugh when I see survival programmes on television today. People are eating raw scorpions and spiders and bugs, including worms. They're all full of rubbish that needs to be removed, and they must be cooked; otherwise you will suffer horrendous illnesses. It's like drinking water straight out of a river or stream that hasn't been boiled or sterilised in some way—a sure way to be heading for disaster.

One of the other things we had to learn on the combat survival course was how to hide and not be found, and how to travel over distances without being seen or drawing attention to yourself in any way by, for instance, lighting fires, smoking, walking on tracks and roads, or visiting areas where people might be. This is how evaders get captured: they are grassed up to the local forces by individuals for reward or self-satisfaction.

Thercfore it is taboo to go anywhere near civilisation. Lofty had a saying, 'High ground is good ground.' It's not like you see on the films, where the person trying to get away is at a railway station and gets stopped and asked for his papers by a policeman or soldier, and if you notice they are always carrying a suitcase with a big umbrella and a hat. This would stand out beyond belief, and not only that but your lack of the knowledge of the language and customs would get you caught. Capture is not an option, as it will be followed without doubt by torture. The captors will try to squeeze out of you what they think you know, so there is always a rule with this one, which is, 'Don't get caught in the first place.'

A series of weekend exercises followed, wherein we had to build shelters out of the local materials that we found in woods and hedgerows, gradually camouflaging them. It would become important, siting your shelter in an area where you wouldn't be found by the casual dog walker or hunter. It is difficult to live in one spot without leaving signs that you are there, like footprints in the mud or evidence of a need for water anywhere, as by a river or stream that you visit. Plus, of course, one has to go to the toilet somewhere, somehow, and this once again attracts animals and birds; even if it is buried, foxes and other animals that like digging may well visit you.

So practise in all these skills was very necessary and would continue for three weeks, and then we would go on the final exercise. We were all taken into a room, stripped naked, and inspected for contraband—and I mean in every orifice. We weren't allowed anything. We were then told to put our boots back on, no socks. All our laces had been removed. We were then each given a pair of Second World War battle-dress trousers, which were very prickly and uncomfortable to wear. These trousers did not have any buttons on them and would be either too small or too large, much to the amusement of the DS staff running the exercise.

We were then each given a battle-dress greatcoat, which once again had no buttons. The sleeves on the one I had were miles too short. We looked like vagrants. I've seen better-dressed tramps in the town. But this was a sign of things to come. We were then issued a button compass, literally the size of a button, that you would have to navigate with, as well as a sketch map that had been hand-drawn and photocopied, with no ground relief. By this I mean you were unable to tell the height of any feature that you would normally see on a map. We were split up into pairs and placed in the back of the four-tonne truck with a tarpaulin. It was closed up behind us, and off we went, to be dropped off somewhere to start the main exercise.

We had to travel across the country to meet an agent—that was the idea. We arrived at our drop-off point and were told by a DS, 'Off you go.' It was dark. All we had was the button compass and this so-called map. I knew straightaway that this would be fun. Off we went into the night, trying to get to the location that was indicated on the map and being aware that there was a hunter force looking for us with dogs—army war dogs, the worst kind. If these dogs got to you and were released from their leads, unless you were very quick at climbing trees or could get to the other side of an impenetrable object, the outcome for you would not be good.

It was raining. It's always raining when this type of exercise is running. There is a saying in the military: 'If it isn't raining, it isn't training.' This was to prepare you for the worst-case scenario. We had no waterproofs, and I remember spotting a scarecrow wearing some fertiliser bags and thinking to myself that they looked like a good set of waterproofs. *Sorry, scarecrow. My need is greater than yours.* I relieved him of them. They worked quite well. At least the rain stayed off me, which kept off the hypothermia, which may well have followed had I got a really bad soaking. We managed to get to the first RV. This is military speak for 'rendezvous point.'

There are rules about these RVs, which I'm not going to go into, as I would in no way want to jeopardise the safety of serving soldiers. However, we were lying in long grass watching this RV when I saw one of the course trainees running downhill with a war dog close on his heels. My immediate thoughts were, *You poor sod*, and behind the dog came several Scottish soldiers, all about five foot two. If they caught him, it would not be pleasant. He would be treated in a most ungentlemanly way. We didn't stick around to find out, but withdrew quickly and left the area in one piece.

This was now a problem. We had to get to the next RV, but how did we know where the RV was? It was clear that the people running the exercise for a bit of realism had grassed up the whereabouts to the hunter force, no doubt much to their amusement, but I for one was not getting captured; this would mean being thrown in puddles, hung from trees by your ankles, thrown in pits full of water, and generally having your life be very miserable for the period of time that they held you, only to be returned to the exercise starting point, which would mean everything would happen again.

I must admit that during this week not a lot was eaten. We were too concerned with not getting captured by the hunter force or eaten by one of those dogs. The weather was bad, the mist was down, and there was a fine rain that guaranteed to get you wet—not pleasant, but you weren't there on a holiday. This was training, training for the real thing. Could you hack it? It depended on whether you had the right stuff. At the end of the fifth day, we met with an agent who gave us a new RV. We were instructed that once we got there, we would find a vehicle in a layby and get into the back of it. *Don't try and escape. It's part of the exercise.*

We moved through several fields and saw a cattle lorry parked in a layby where the RV had been indicated. We went to it and climbed in the back, and there inside were many others. All had stories to tell of their adventures and how they had evaded capture over the last week. Some had clearly fared better than others. The truck drove off. We hadn't gone far when it stopped, and I heard voices, Scottish voices, opening the back of the truck and telling us to get out, in the most unpleasant manner. We were all thrown up against this truck and poked and prodded, searched for contraband. I remember I'd found a woollen jumper, and I had one of the pockets that I'd ripped off of it and put on my head to keep warm. It had worked perfectly until an officer from the hunter force removed it unceremoniously from my head. I looked at him with the contempt he deserved.

He said to me, 'What's your name?' I looked at him and gave him the textbook answer: 'I can't answer that question.' I could have told him who I was: number, rank, name, date of birth were all I was allowed to give. Say nothing, sign nothing, but number, rank, name, date of birth—that's as far as it went, no matter what they did to you, no matter what they told you.

We were taken away in vehicles to some buildings where we were to be interrogated, which involved sleep deprivation. You stood against the wall on your tiptoes (boots removed) and on fingertips in what they call the stress position. This would go on for hours and hours, and occasionally you'd be dragged away for interrogation, all the time wearing a hood and being subjected to white noise. Many cracked. They couldn't hack it. It went on and on and on, the interrogation, the sleep deprivation, the lack of food, the constant attempts to get information out of us their way, and all you gave was, number, rank, name, date of birth. There was no way any other information was coming out of me. I was not going to betray anyone.

You end up not knowing where you are or whether it's day or night. You are so tired, you haven't eaten for the week you've been on the run, and now their attempts to beat you down, break you, get you to give information,: *Who were you with? What were you doing? What unit are you in? What was your mission? Where are the others?* Never, never ever, would I talk.

They were looking for special people, people that could stand the pace and not give in. Clearly, in reality there would have been a time when their methods made the human body give in, being able to take only so much punishment. So you would have to have a cover story ready that could not be checked, to justify why you were there. Hopefully this would be accepted and you would be sent off to some camp where escape, either on the way or there, would be possible, as your priority was to escape at any opportunity—to go.

Having said this, there is a motto that says, 'Don't get caught in the first place.'

Eventually, I was dragged into an interrogation room and thrown onto a chair. My hood was removed, and there sat looking at me one of the directing staff, wearing a white armband. He said to me, 'It's okay. It's over.' He pushed a cup of tea towards me. I wouldn't take it. I wouldn't talk to him. I wouldn't acknowledge him. No eye contact. I just looked down. I suppose at this stage I was partly delirious—no sleep or food for over a week. I wasn't sure really where I was or who anyone was, but most of all, I trusted no one. He said to me again, 'It's over. You can talk to me now.' And then he gave me a sentence that we had been told would signal it was okay to talk to them.

I still didn't trust him. I'd come all this way. I wasn't going to get caught out now, not at this stage. I wanted this and wanted it so bad. He looked at me again, and I knew him. He was wearing a white armband. He said the sentence to me again, pushing the tea towards me. I looked at him and I knew he was telling the truth. It was all over. I had passed.

I had passed another major obstacle on the course, but there were several that hadn't, and they were returned to their units, having failed. The next obstacle was the army parachute course. I'd had experience at parachuting briefly in the sport leisure roll in Cyprus. I had only made a couple of jumps and couldn't say honestly that I was in love with it. Military parachuting is not the same as you see on the television, where people do forward rolls out of light aircraft wearing pink suits, little glasses on and massive watches and little packs on their backs. In the military it is certainly not like that, as anyone reading this who has been through the military parachute course will tell you.

13

THE PARACHUTE COURSE

We arrived at the course at Brize Norton, in Oxfordshire, and there was trouble from day one. We had a parachute regiment RSM in charge of the course. He did not like SAS and he showed it. We had just come off the combat survival course on Sunday. This was now Monday morning, only one day since coming out of interrogation. All our kits were filthy, boots white instead of black—all the polish having been washed out of them through running over the mountains—and we were still suffering from sleep deprivation, but we were supposed to be bright as buttons, ready to start this parachute course. In fact we looked like vagrants who had been picked up off the streets. However, this was unrecognised by the RSM. He expected bull and lots of it.

Unfortunately for him, he was looking in the wrong place. This was the last thing on our minds. We were still on the course. We were surviving. We were picked on at every opportunity by him. Our hair was long compared to the rest of the army, but as most of us would work in Northern Ireland, we had been told not to get it cut. We were there to learn to parachute and that was all. We didn't need to know drill; we'd already done that for many years at our battalions. However, he didn't look at it that way.

We started our training. We hung from harnesses in hangars, sticking our arms out in different directions. We rolled on mats to the left, to the right, backwards, forwards, every which way, being constantly told, 'Feet and knees together. Take the landing that comes.' We heard it in our sleep.

They had an interesting device called a fan. It was a big wheel with wire on it. You had a harness on and you had to jump out of a doorway from a wooden mock-up aircraft.

This training went on and on for another four weeks of the course. We were at the mercy of the RAF in the daytime and a mad para RSM every other time. It just couldn't get any better. Everywhere we went we saw the sign, 'Knowledge Dispels Fear.' Never mind this; we just wanted to get it over with. This was one of those things we had to do.

We completed all our ground training, and then came the day of our first proper parachute jump. This would be from a balloon or zeppelin, the same type that had protected London during the Second World War, with a basket hanging underneath. It wasn't like the hot air balloons you would see people going for joyrides in around the countryside. It was certainly no joyride for us. We drew and fitted our parachutes, mark-four steerable. However, these were equipped with Capewells, which you could pull the covers off of, then insert your thumbs into the D-rings and pull. This would cut away the main canopy, allowing you to clear a malfunction parachute and pull your reserve. The first four climbed aboard the balloon basket. It was square-shaped, and one person stood in each corner. You hooked up your static line to the centre of the balloon. There was a PJI (parachute jump instructor) with you who controlled a metal bar across the entrance to the front of the basket you would jump from. The word was given: 'Up eight hundred feet, four men jumping.' This I can only describe as an attempt at suicide from a tall building. Once we got up to eight hundred feet, the basket would stop, and the instructor would look over the side to the ground and look for a man waving a green flag. This indicated that it was clear to jump.

We were called forward one at a time. The bar was lifted up and we were told to place our hands over the reserve parachute, which was in front of us, and then the order was given: 'Off you go.' Oh dear, what an experience. Everyone who stood there said to the PJI, 'Don't say it, shout it. Make it like a word of command and I'll go.' He did, and off we went. You fell three hundred feet before your parachute opened, and then it would collapse and open again. They call this breathing. To this day I am sure that if anything had gone wrong, we would not have been able to correct it in time. That would have been the end. What an experience.

I landed on the ground and attempted a parachute roll. I was like a sack of potatoes falling off the back of a lorry. What a mess. However, I walked away from it in one piece. They say any jump you walk away from is a good jump. We all did one, and then to our horror we had to go up and do it all over again. I've spoken to many people who are currently serving in the parachute regiment, and they tell me that they have never done a balloon jump. It's too costly to get them out, and not only that, but they can't go up in wind because they may just blow away, as they are huge devices that have to be filled with helium. Lucky them.

So, two jumps completed. Eight in all had to be done to get your wings. An aircraft now followed, the C-130 Hercules, a big transporter, the workhorse of the Royal Air Force. We started off doing what they call clean fatigue, in single sticks of six; this means six men going out of one door, port or starboard, one after the other, only wearing a main parachute and a reserve and no equipment. This we did and walked away from it. All was going well, and then we progressed to two sticks of six jumping simultaneously port and starboard, and then jumping with equipment; this meant you had a sixty-pound weight fixed to the front of your harness for training. This took the shape of a jerry can filled with sand, called a container, which speeded up your descent considerably. Once you cleared the aircraft and checked your canopy, and hopefully all was well, you lowered your equipment on a fifteen-foot suspension line below you.

I was on the first drop with equipment. I cleared the aircraft, got my canopy, and lowered my equipment after checking for other parachutists to my left and right. I landed okay. I started packing my parachute in the green para bag, kneeling between my chute and container, and then I heard the words, 'Container away,' over the megaphone that the DZ safety officer was using. We had not been trained for this. What was happening? I didn't know, and I looked up and saw a parachutist trying to fly his reserve chute whilst in twists. He had cut his container away to slow down his descent. This meant he had released it from the fifteen-foot suspension line that was hanging below him. It was now in free flight, heading towards me.

I got up and started to run off the DZ (drop zone) fast, looking back as I ran. I heard a thud. I stopped and looked back. The sixty-pound jerry can had landed right where I had been kneeling packing my chute. It sunk into the ground at least four inches flat and jumped back up in the air, landing on the other side of my reserve some four feet away. If I had not run, I would have gone to Spirit that day. Once again I was being looked after; Spirit told me what to do.

To complete this course we had to do night jumps, as well as a jump from a full aircraft of sixty-four parachutists all leaving the aircraft at the same time using the port and starboard jump doors, in the sequence of one port, one starboard, one port, one starboard, until the aircraft was empty of parachutists. This was a fairly fast way of doing it. However, it could go wrong; if port and starboard came out at the same time, they would collide at the rear of the aircraft and entanglement would follow as they descended to the ground. The results could vary.

I got my parachute wings.

14

RETURN TO HEREFORD FROM THE PARACHUTE COURSE

On return to Hereford we were sent for by the training major, Major Hopkins, known as Hoppe. This man would sort out any problems you had. He was well-respected. He knew how to deal with units that gave their soldiers a hard time. With regard to selection, his job was to head the training wing of the regiment and get people through on the administration side. However, he was never to be crossed, if you knew what was good for you.

He got all of us that had just completed the parachute course in his office and said, 'Well done. You have been accepted for service with the regiment.' The proudest day of my life—well, I thought, because it was just at that moment when a man to the right of me said, 'I want to go back to my unit.' The tension in the office was indescribable. We all thought we were hearing things. Somebody who had just gone through the SAS selection course wanted to return to his unit. Unbelievable!

There was this long pause. Hoppe said, 'What did you say? You want to return to your unit? You mean to tell me that you have messed my staff around for the last five months, and now, at the end of it all, you want to go back to your unit?' This was not good. The man stood next to me. I was now in the limelight, where I didn't want to be. Everyone was looking at me, as he was standing next to me. Hoppe said, 'What did you do it for, if you had no intention of joining the regiment?'

The man said he'd wanted to see if he could do it, and he had proved it to himself. Now he wanted to go back to his unit. And then came the statement that I had been dreading. Hoppe said to me, 'Bob, take him back to the bashers and get his head sorted out, and don't come back until you have.' Brilliant. Now I was in it. Why me? After all that work. No, the anger wasn't aimed directly at me, but you had to be a grey man whilst on selection, not getting singled out for anything unless it was good, and this certainly wasn't. I left the room with him and went back to the bashers. We sat on a bed and I said to him, 'All that we went through, I don't believe you. You want to go back to your unit? It's the last place in the world I want to be.'

I had a mission. That mission was to get this man's head right. I couldn't go back to Hoppe and say I'd failed, so I pleaded and pleaded with him. 'Just give it a go,' I said. 'You mean to tell me after all we went through on that parachute course that you want to throw your hand in? I don't believe it.' I said, 'What an achievement. We are going now to get badged by the CO. Just give it a go.' We were there some time. This went on. I didn't believe it. I pleaded with him. Eventually he caved in and said, 'All right, then. I'll give it six months. If I don't like it, I'm off.'

I said, 'Well, that's fine. This way you would have given it a go, and if you didn't like it no one could say anything.' We went back to the office and knocked on the door. 'Come' was the reply. The others were still standing there. He made them wait for our decision—not good, more sideways glances. I looked at them and shrugged my shoulders as if to say, *Don't blame me. It wasn't my fault.* I had just been invited to join the finest fighting force in the world, and I wasn't ever going to turn that down, ever. 'Well, what have you decided?'

I said before he could get a word in, 'He's staying, sir.'
And the answer came, 'And I should think so. Right. I've sorted the others out for what squadrons they are going to. You two are going to B Squadron, and they are in Ireland. Okay?'

'Yes, sir.'
Hoppe got up from his chair. 'Right. At last, let's go,' he said. We opened the door for him and out he went. We followed him like lost sheepdogs, but we were proud because we knew that we were going to the CO's office to get badged into the regiment.

15

THE CO'S OFFICE

We were taken over to meet the commanding officer to get badged. The famous beige beret and winged dagger cap badge were mine at last. I had waited for this moment for many years. I couldn't believe it had actually arrived. Here I was, about to be taken into the brotherhood of the finest fighting force in the world and into its history, way back in the desert in the Second World War, where Colonel David Stirling had formed this elite fighting force that had carried on and taken his great name into the future. There were many stories in the regimental history of his deeds and daring—that he would often take on overwhelming odds to achieve his aim, all in the name of, 'Who dares, wins.'

We went to the adjutant's office. Hoppe went in. The door was all glass, so you could see the adjutant get up and come outside with Hoppe. They turned right and walked towards the commanding officer's door. The adjutant knocked. We heard, 'Come.' The adjutant went in, followed by Hoppe and us. The commanding officer, the man in charge of the SAS, was there. We were face-to-face. He wanted us. We had passed all his tests. It was all first names. We were in the big boys' league now. We were given respect for who we were and what we had achieved.

One hundred eighty of us had been called forward, but only eighteen had passed, and several of those would be RTU in the first year; just because we got into this regiment didn't mean we would survive. We would all have to serve one year as troopers, not on specialist pay but on pay at the rank we'd been at in our previous units. We had to pass a skills course within the first twelve months to qualify for SAS pay.

The office had a desk with its back to the wall, not the window. There was a leather armchair in front of it. You didn't march in here or salute like you did in other commanding officers' offices; you came in and took a seat, a comfy seat, and discussed the situation that had brought you there. This could be good or bad, but it was the way things were dealt with. You had a say. You weren't guilty before you went in, like you were in many other units. Things were to be discussed, and if you had been wronged, it would be put right. However, if you were in the wrong, you would have to pay normally—this meant financially; otherwise, if it were really severe, you could even be RTU. It depended on the situation.

The commanding officer introduced himself with his first name and his last name—completely different from anything I'd seen before. He shook our hands, all of us welcomed to the regiment. After a brief chat in which he did the talking, he handed us one at a time, with a handshake, the famous beret, and sewn on it was the cloth badge of the winged dagger, the most famous regimental badge in the British Army, if not the world. And I had just been given it. You can imagine how I felt. All the doubters had been wrong; I had what it took. My mother could eat her own words. My OC back in the battalion could do the same. I'd made it.

I now know what it's like to win an Olympic gold medal. You stand there, and they raise the flag of your country, and you're in the number-one position. I could relate to that on this day. It was a feeling that not many soldiers will ever feel, this achievement being for the few and only the few who could get past the selection course. You had to be outstanding. That is the only word I can find to describe it. And I always say any man who can pass that selection course can't be bad; he has a will to win, which is only found in the very few.

I can only repeat what I've said before. There is a motto within the SAS that says, 'Many are called forward, but only a few are chosen.'

The door was opened and we filed out one at a time. No one spoke. We looked around at the regimental headquarters. We hadn't been there before. It was busy, with the clerks all over the place, telephones ringing, messages and notepaper being handed to others. You could see that a lot went on here. Now we were part of it.

We walked out of the building into the daylight and put our berets on. They needed shrinking. by this I mean immersing the beret in water, wringing it out and then shaping it to your head by putting it on and pulling it down on one side, you did this with a brand-new beret. These were standard-issue, not the best. However, I would save this one and buy another one when I was down in Aldershot, from a company called Victor's. They made the best berets. They shrunk just right to fit your head properly, and why not? To be proud, to show all that you were wearing this famous beret and what you had achieved.

We all went back to Hoppe's office. He said, 'Well done, once again. Welcome to the regiment. You will need stable belts. I have some here.' He produced a box with brand-new blue belts, the chrome buckle with the famous winged dagger in the centre. I purchased one straightaway.

You had to have it, as it was part of your uniform. I adjusted it and put it on. We were then issued our travel documents to get us to Northern Ireland. We were told to pack our kit and what time transport left the guard room.

As I walked out of Hoppe's office, I ran into my DS. His name was Tony. He said I looked like a brand-new trouper. I said, 'Yes, I know. Thank you.' And I put my hand out and shook his. He'd had the power through the selection course to get rid of me, but he hadn't. He was a true soldier doing a good job. He said very few words, but when he did, they could cut like a knife. The regiment needed people like him to carry out the tasks they were given, and I was proud to be one of them.

16

B SQUADRON

We were issued our travel documents and sent over to the clothing store to draw additional equipment and prepare to go off and join our squadron. Transport was arranged, and the next day off we went.

I had no special training. There wasn't time, and who would I do it with? Everyone went there with weeks of extensive training to prepare them for what they might meet. I had to learn on the job, and I did. This was easy, as I was thrown in at the deep end straightaway with a lot of people that were quite laid-back about the job. All units in the British Army have their characters, some funny, some not so funny. There were certainly plenty of both around. I was looked upon as a new boy even though I had many years of experience in Northern Ireland on the streets and in the rural areas.

When I met the rest of the squadron, my psychic side kicked in. I remember going into the interest room where everyone was waiting for a talk from the OC. I went in first with the other new arrival that had come with me. I remember my initial thoughts. I had expected grown men in their thirties and forties, experienced. What a shock. At first I thought, *What have I done?* I had just spent the last five months trying to reach the standard of these people that I wanted to be part of, and I was shocked by what I saw. There were lots of them in their twenties. I instantly started analysing them, one by one, and realised what a mixed bag there was. It was clear that some of the people who had just been RTU from my selection would have fit better in that room, especially some of the paras and marines who were clearly dedicated soldiers and knew their stuff, because it was obvious to me a lot of the people that I was looking at didn't. And this would be proved to me over the years to come.

Some of the senior ranks, at sergeant and above, were left over from the days when the regiment had fought on the side of the sultan of Oman during Operation Storm. The regiment had played a major part in maintaining the sultan's kingdom in Oman and fighting off the commonest insurgents trying to take the country from him. This secret war had been a great success for the regiment, and many men had excelled and shown true bravery, often against overwhelming numbers, especially in my own troop, Eight Troop, B Squadron. They had defended the Fort at Marbat, and several distinguished awards had been given to members of the troop who had fought bravely for their lives against a massive enemy force and survived, leaving many of the enemy dead.

On completion of Operation Storm, the sultan had asked to set up a special force equivalent to the SAS and offered jobs to members of the regiment to man this unit. This was done, and they were highly paid. The British Army was poorly paid at the time, and unfortunately a lot of the cream of the regiment had left to do this, and very successfully, too.

This had to have an effect somewhere, and it did. A lot of the senior people who left the regiment also left empty spaces for command and control, which had to be filled by members who would have otherwise probably not achieved these ranks. I saw this firsthand and sometimes to my disappointment, but fortunately a lot of those people were coming to the end of their service and would be replaced by others.

The problem was that what had been required in the days of the Malayan emergency, when the regiment had fought so bravely, were men, big men, who could carry heavy loads long-distance over mountains and dense jungle. The regiment called them 'trigger pullers.' These were good soldiers and not always going to rise to the level of command. Many of these men were still serving when I joined, and they hadn't had the training that was then standard in the army.

I was receiving a briefing for an operation, this should be carried out by what is known as formal orders, these are a sequence of orders with subheadings delivered with the use of models made out on the ground using various objects. Every section commander and platoon sergeant would have a model kit in a tobacco tin with him at all times so he could deliver a good set of orders. But this particular set of orders was being delivered by one of these trigger pullers who had clearly been promoted above his capabilities, they weren't good, there was so much left out, no one really knew what they were doing.

All NCOs—the section commanders and platoon sergeants, of course—in the British Army were going to the school of infantry for weapons instructor training and tactics training. I'd been there and done these courses with the battalion. The men I was now working with hadn't, and it showed. However, like anyone new to a job, I kept quiet, looked, and learned, and when the opportunity arose, I showed my skills.

I had to learn surveillance skills, this involved foot surveillance, car surveillance and covert OP's I hadn't been shown any of this, I had to join in with the operation that was going on at the time and just watch and learn, I had also been given no training on pistols in the form of covert carry, this I had to be shown on a range day with live ammunition, no time for training. There were many new skills to be learnt and because of the lack of this training I initially felt I was looked down upon by the other members of the troop but I explained to them that I had come straight from selection and hadn't any build up training unlike everyone else I hadn't done the one month pre-Northern Ireland course where all these skills are practiced before flying over to Ireland.

I enjoyed my time in Northern Ireland. At last I was doing a worthwhile job. We were there to aid the civil power, which involved politicians and police, and to help bring peace to Northern Ireland. I'm not sure whether the aim was achieved, as they now have a wonderful free country to live in, acts of terrorism aren't what they were, and people can walk the streets once again without feeling like they are living in some cowboy film that you've seen on the television, as that's how it was. I found the people of Northern Ireland to be some of the nicest, most hospitable, comical people you could wish to meet. Many billions of pounds have been put into that country to give them a better life, but unfortunately it cost the lives of many, on both sides.

I just hope that sense is seen out there and that the guns and the bombs are rejected and replaced by goodwill and give-and-take, and that they put hatred to one side. There is a saying, 'Forgive and forget.' I would say forgive but never forget. Why? To make sure it never happens again, and an example of this is what happened in the Second World War in Europe. After all, Europe lives together today, and people can get on if they really want to. I wish all the people of Northern Ireland love and light.

17

NATIONAL COUNTERTERRORIST TEAM

On return to Hereford we were to take on our next role. For the next six months we were assigned to the national counterterrorist team. This was early 1980. If there was a local problem, you would ring 999 and expect the police, ambulance, or fire brigade to attend to your problem. Well, if there was a terrorist incident in this country, the national counterterrorist team would deal with it, and as you would expect, it was the country's blue-light service, just like your local services always on call, always ready, highly trained, and very effective against any terrorist organisation that wanted to perform in this country. My advice to the terrorists was, 'Don't even think about it.'

This was good for me. The training started from scratch. Everyone started at day one again and went through everything in depth. At last I would be trained to the same level as everyone else in the squadron. I was also sent off to what was known as the fast-drive course. This was with the police. We were basically training to be police drivers, the type you see on our motorways in the big Volvos, but in our case it was white Range Rovers. For the role we were filling, we needed them. I would have to drive one of these with five people with all the standard equipment at possibly 120 miles an hour if necessary, blue lights and sirens on, to get my team members to our destination, wherever it was in the country.

I found this most enjoyable. The vehicles were fitted with roll cages and run-flat tyres. We were all strapped in, in case things went wrong. We learned to drive in convoy, using radios to communicate on the country roads and A roads so we could overtake on blind bends knowing full well nothing was coming the other way, as the front car was clearing the way. It was quite interesting to see the faces of some road users when five Range Rovers all driving on the wrong side of the road overtook at once on a blind bend and got away with it. They must have thought we were mad, but we were safe because we had a front car giving instructions.

I was trained as an assault team member. These are men that go into the building where the terrorists are located and clear the rooms—the sharp end of the job, as you've seen on the films and television, giving the bad guys the good news. Never shooting a hostage—this was what the training was about. Picking out the good from the bad and dealing with the situation that you found yourself in at the time.

I was also trained as a sniper, both day and night. The use of night observation equipment was important in the training to see and not be seen. 'Surprise' was always the word.

After a series of exercises confirming the team were ready to take on the role, finally we took over the national counterterrorist team responsibilities. Every day was training, long and hard, and no stone went unturned. We were ready, should the call come, and in May 1980 it did. We were just coming back from training. It was lunchtime, and the troop sergeant, Roy, said to us, 'The Iranian Embassy in London has been taken over by a group of terrorists. We are on standby to go.' And we were ready. We were always ready. The kits were always packed to go. We were given the word to deploy to London.

There were hostages being held in the building at Princes Gate in London. There were several terrorists, all armed, holding them. They had even taken a policeman from the front door, holding him hostage. This had never happened in England before, but since the Munich Olympics and the disaster that had happened there, we'd had a team. This team was from the best unit in the British Army, the SAS, and I'm sure to this day that had the terrorists known of our existence, this incident would have never happened. They wouldn't have dared to try this. We have a saying in the military: 'Prior planning and preparation prevents piss-poor performance.' They hadn't followed this rule.

That night we moved into position in the building next door to the Iranian embassy to await the outcome of negotiations. If they failed, we were the next card to be played. There was a television programme on at the time. where competitors went over an assault course, and to get double points they could play their joker card if the competitors felt they were good at one particular subject that the game demanded. This card was held by the government that day, and unfortunately, I knew what would happen. I thought, *They're not going to let sixty rottweilers loose in London, are they?, by this I mean the SAS*

117

We had been there for five days in all. Negotiations went on and on. I was convinced that this would all end in a peaceful settlement., The terrorists didn't know what was sitting next door, and if they had, I think they would have given up fast.

Suddenly a report came through: *They've shot a hostage*. Oh my god. This changed everything. Madness. Why would they do that? I knew that the police could not handle this situation anymore, and that control would be handed over to the military. And then, later, more madness—*They've shot another one*. At this point the government signed over control of the incident to the military. A procedure that was put in place at the time and is still operative today. And then the words we were waiting for came: *All stations, this is nine. I have control.* This was the commanding officer on his radio to all call signs, confirming that control had in fact been handed over to the military. We were going in.

In the military you have a series of points you move to before an attack, or in this case, an assault on a position. The first move is to your FUP, 'forming up point,' and then to your start line. From this point the advance towards the intended location begins. Well, at the Iranian Embassy, movement from one position to the other was communicated by code words. These words were taken from location names in London. One was 'London Bridge.' The first code word came—gas masks on, weapons ready. I did not believe it. This was London. It couldn't happen here. Were they really going to set sixty rottweilers loose in the capital? Then came the second code word. I think it was something like 'Hyde Park.' We were going in. I knew this because at that location we would be in sight of the public—no turning back.

18

THE ASSAULT

We moved forward. We were in assault teams of two men per team, and we all had jobs to do. First of all, we had to get in. This would be achieved by blowing an entry point at the rear of the building using explosives. It would be an electronic initiation. However, if the explosives failed to detonate, my job was to run forward and gain entry with a sledgehammer.

My team's final assault position was behind a small wall that we all had to lie down behind. It could not have been more than two feet high, which would not be much cover from a big blast. We waited for the big bang. It did not happen. Instead I got a slap on the head from one of the team. *Go, go.* I thought it must have been a misfire.

A misfire occurs when there is a problem with the circuit or when the detonator fails to explode and set off the main charge. Whatever had gone wrong, it was now up to me to get us in. I got up and ran forward. The explosives were still there on a long, flat length of wood leaning against the wall. Well, consider this: I thought that it was a misfire. The safety time for an electronic initiation misfire is ten minutes; this means you don't go near a device that has been attempted electronically for ten minutes.

Well, it was obvious that we did not have time to hang around and wait, so I kicked the charge out of my way, thinking, *Well, if it goes off, I won't know anything about it. I'll be all over the park.* And then I started to make an entry point through the window to my front. It had wooden shutters behind it, which were closed, and heavy draped curtains behind those. It didn't take me long, as obviously the adrenaline was rushing. I made an entry point. I remember removing the safety catch on my MP5 submachine gun with my thumb. Ready to deal with the aggressor that I might now meet inside, I climbed in. We were in.

Rooms were cleared of terrorists one at a time and hostages were handed out to the rear of the building. All had to be IDed and the opposition dealt with. Regrettably, a fire had been started, so we had to get out as soon as the task was completed, which we did.

Ground floor cleared, I linked up on the first floor with Derek, another team member who had just been in a life-threatening situation and resolved it on his own. This man was a totally professional soldier and a man I would not have hesitated to do any job with, no matter what. There are soldiers, and then there are men like Derek, very rare.

We were back next door, our task had been completed, we had saved all the remaining hostages and captured one terrorist, the other terrorists died due to their actions. Unfortunately the Embassy caught fire but this was brought under control and today it has been rebuilt to be as grand as it ever was. . ' .

At the end of this we all made statements, and on our return to Hereford, months later, it was announced that two QGMs were to be awarded for the embassy action. When the names were published and Derek and I were not on the list, we just said, 'Well, never mind.' It would have been nice to have that medal, but obviously we hadn't shouted loud enough. But then it wasn't about medals; it was about saving lives. And I think we had done this quite well. I'm sure Spirit was with me that day, looking after me. Thank you, Spirit.

It would have been nice to meet Her Majesty the Queen in her home. It looks quite nice on the telly.

Many books have been written on this incident, and I remember that just after it happened the Met Police firearms team, D11, as it was then, said that they should have the counterterrorist team role, not the SAS, as they could do the job. Well, what a statement. The SAS soldier is in a totally different league from any UK police officer. They are exceptional individuals, Great Britain's finest, who may be copied but will not be equalled.

The Iranian Embassy, London, 1980. This picture shows ropes being prepared on the roof of the Iranian Embassy for abseilers to come down and land on the various balconies to the rear of the building. Notice the white ropes; these ropes are no longer used, as they tended to snag in descenders and were only 11 millimeters thick. The new rope used is 13 millimeters, which does not snag. Also, the use of the leg bag came from this incident.

This picture shows Bob entering a rear window of the Iranian Embassy. He has one leg through the window after smashing his way in with a sledgehammer. If you look to his right you can see a four-inch-wide wooden plank with masking tape around it. This was the charge (explosive) that was supposed to blow this entry through and could not be set off due to the abseilers coming down. Bob smashed his way through to get the rest of the team in.

The picture that the world has seen many times. In front of the Iranian Embassy as an assault team effects entry by explosive charge. Inside this area was the chief terrorist as well as PC Trevor Lock and Sim Harris, the BBC sound recordist. vUnfortunately for him, the chief terrorist never made it out alive. However, the other three lives were saved by men who were highly trained and knew their job inside out, going under the motto of SAS (Speed, Aggression, Surprise).

19

THE FALKLANDS WAR, 1982

T he news came to the world: 'Argentina Invades the Falkland Islands.' Most people thought that the Falklands were up around the top of Scotland somewhere, not down at the bottom of the southern Atlantic Ocean. Whoever went there, and why? How did British people live there? Well, they did, and Argentina weren't just going to stomp in there and take over. Who do you think you are, Mr Argy?

The powers that be decided, *Well, we'll show them. We are coming to take the islands back.* Planning started. So did training. There was one problem: no maps.

Yes, no maps. How could you plan a war with no maps? Then a breakthrough—someone had been there on a holiday and taken photos, plus he had a map. All was saved. He was invited to give us all a briefing on the islands.

He arrived. He was a serving staff sergeant in some unit. Well, he should have had his act together, as he knew what was expected. However, it turned out that his map was a tourist map of places of interest to visit. His photos were all of penguins. Brilliant. What more would we need to know? Things weren't looking good on the planning side.

The government decided they had to be seen doing something: *Send a task force now.* And we did. We put everything that we might need on ships and set sail. Off we went, the fleet full of Paras, Marines, Guardsmen, and Gurkhas, as well as big guns and ammo. You name it, they put it on the ships. No maps? Sort that out later.

What about us, the SAS? We needed to get OPs (observation posts) and see what was going on, what the Argies were up to. Standard practice in war is to get eyes on the ground. My squadron was given the task and told to prepare for it. We trained and trained and trained.

Eventually we were ready,, as part of this training we had to all get on a C-130 one night. We had two C-130s, also known as Hercules transport planes, we were going to land at a military airport at night unannounced to test the airfield's radar and alertness. Our pilots would be wearing PNG night vision. As we approached the military airfield one aircraft followed closely by the other, we were coming into land when suddenly the first aircraft put on full power and went into a steep climb. The second aircraft at the last moment when realising the situation that was in front of him did exactly the same, I was in the second aircraft. We all ended up at the other end of the plane in a heap. I had been sitting on a motorbike, ready to roar off the back with another bike and go to a specific location at the airfield. Well, there we were in a big heap—bikes, bodies, and equipment. Nice.

What had happened? Well, as the two aircraft were about to cross the air-field perimeter fence, the first pilot had realised he was too low and that we were about to hit the fence—hence the sudden power on and steep climb and the second pilot realising the same situation followed him. Spirit had been with me once again, in a big way. Thank you, Spirit.

I'm not going to go into the details of SAS operations in the Falklands, as in no way do I want to jeopardise future SAS missions by revealing their tactics, but I will give you the funny side of some things.

We moved out to Ascension Island, unloaded all the kit—lots of it—prepared for the task, sorted the ammo—lots of ammo—loaded the planes, hurried up, and waited. I'd been here before. The waiting went on. We were keen to go..

And then we loaded the planes and loaded the planes, loaded the planes again, unloaded the planes, each time at different locations, with different ideas. Were we ever going to do this? Back to hurry up and wait.

Then, suddenly, bad news: a chopper had gone into the sea, eighteen men on board, most of them SAS. What? This couldn't be. All dead. Who were they?. What had happened? Well, it appeared that they had been cross decking, which is moving from one ship to the next. It was the last lift of the day and dark, tactical, so there hadn't been any lights on, pilots probably on PNGs. The helicopter had been about to land on the deck of the second ship. Take into consideration the up and down movement of the ship due to the sea.

As the helicopter was coming down to land on the deck, the ship was going up—collision. Boat hits helicopter, helicopter falls down the side of the ship, and ship comes back down—no chance, a disaster. I knew one man who had survived. I'd done selection with him.

His name was Alex. He told me the story later, back in Hereford. I'd lost a lot of friends that day, including squadron leader Garth Hawkins. He was FAC (forward air controller) for the regiment. I had been working with him only months before the war. You could not get a better soldier. The very sad thing about the crash was that most of the senior ranks of the regiment were on board; this took a lot of the command and control from the squadrons.

And to my devastation, I'd also lost my friend Geordie, who I had met and spent a week with back in Norway, with the battalion. He was one of the reasons I'd joined the SAS.

Things were not going well. People were keen to do something, anything, just to get off Ascension Island and go to war. Missions were planned and then cancelled—not good. Too much sitting around. The SSM (squadron sergeant major) would organise another run up the green mountain. We were getting bored. And the flies were everywhere, millions of them. You would go to meals and discover that the flies had beaten you to it. So it was compo (army rations) or nothing. And there were the land crabs, everywhere, millions of them, and yes, they nipped—not just any nip. They hung on hard. Try getting one off your finger—not easy.

Eventually the hanging around and waiting ended, the word came through. We were going south at last It had been decided that we would join the other squadrons on the Falkland Islands this involved a parachute entry into the theatre of operation and the only way this could be done was what is known as a water jump where you parachute into the sea and because this was an operational theatre it had to be done at night.

The jump would be from 650 feet with no reserve chute, you only had one chance. Because of the nature of the jump and the water temperature we would be wearing divers dry bags which is a rubber suit that you climb into and zip up by a diagonal zip either across your back or front. Around the collar and cuffs of the sleeves there was thick tight rubber which was designed to make the suit watertight onto your body.

We would be jumping on mark five steerable chutes and also wearing a PLP (parachutist life preserver) which was a life jacket uninflated and designed that when you hit the water you would pull a chord at the bottom and it would inflate, also there is a salt water activated light on it to indicate your location in the water. All equipment, weapons, clothing, Bergens, personal ammunition and rations would be packed and then placed into plastic bags, sealed and loaded into boxes, large boxes wrapped in polythene and fixed to pallets. When these boxes were complete they would contain several soldier's equipment. They would be fitted with several parachutes and then rolled off the tailgate of a Hercules C-130, the parachutes on the containers would be connected to the aircraft on a static line, the idea being that once the container left the aircraft, the chutes would deploy automatically and sail down gently, this was the theory behind it. The parachutists would jump separately after the heavy drop, safety would have to be observed as it would not be good to drop these heavy containers into the water whilst parachutists were floating about.

So the process began, all the equipment was packed, waterproofed as best as possible and loaded onto the aircraft, parachutes were attached to the equipment, the time had come, we were going to war at last. All the troops that were going to parachute climbed onto the aircraft, due to the amount of equipment that was going to be dropped there wasn't a lot of room for the troops so you sat where you could and away we went up into the air heading towards the Falkland Islands.

It was a long journey, many cups of tea were drank from white plastic disposable cups and the RAF feed you on these aircraft from a white cardboard box which looks like one you would get from a cake shop when you buy half a dozen cream cakes, inside you would find sandwiches wrapped in clingfilm which included spam plus cheese and onion, the onion would be a ring of sliced raw onion, there would be the standard bag of plain Walkers crisps, a tin of fizzy drink and a chocolate bar, normally a Kit-Kat or Mars bar. Several of these would be distributed to you during your journey, the toilet facilities on these transport aircraft aren't the best, there is a white toilet bowl which looks like a tin at the rear of the aircraft on the ramp, for privacy there is a curtain which can be pulled round. On flushing the toilet, no water appears there is just a loud sucking noise, I suspect that what you have just done has just been dispatched into the atmosphere, I can only imagine as I have no knowledge of where it goes!

Finally the word comes that we are in the area of the jump, dry bags on, parachutes on, check each others equipment, there will be two passes, the first on is the heavy drop of equipment and the second one is the parachutists, the load masters are in position, the tailgate opens, we are now on redlights only inside, there are no wing lights flashing, nothing to know we are here, the pilots are flying on night vision goggles. The red light comes on, green light, the heavy drop goes off the ramp, watching it go, suddenly 'disaster', the parachutes haven't deployed, they have snapped straight off the containers, they haven't been rigged properly and now the containers are heading towards the sea in free fall. They hit the water and sank instantly, everything was lost, no weapons, no equipment, no ammunition, no rations, no Bergens, belt kit, nothing, it was now all in the bottom of the South Atlantic. Every container that went off the back of the Hercules did exactly the same.

The responsibility for the rigging of these containers was down to air dispatch, a specialist unit who are responsible for all the rigging of containers, vehicles and anything else that is dropped by parachute out of the back of an aircraft. They would have practiced for years to get this right but on the day when it was most needed they let us down. The aircraft circled, approached the drop zone again in what's know as running in, our parachutes all hooked up to the static line, it would be a tailgate exit from the aircraft, red light, green light, go! Clear the aircraft, check your canopy, make sure you can get your head back and see that your canopy is fully inflated and then look around you for other parachutists who may be dangerously close, the last thing you want is an entanglement with another parachute. Because the height was only 650 feet for the jump the water approaches quickly, the rule is when you are approximately 50-30 feet from the water you raise your hand and lift up one of the covers on the Capewell on the riser of you parachute, this is located on your shoulders where you will find a ring, you place your thumb in the ring and at the appropriate time; 50 – 30 feet from the water you pull the ring, this will release one of the risers, these are webbing straps attached to both your shoulders that have rigging lines attached to them, there are so many of equal amounts on either side, this will also deflate your parachute, accelerating you into the water, however if you don't carry out this procedure there is a danger of the whole parachute canopy coming down over the top of you, you would then be entangled in rigging lines and parachute and there is a very strong possibility that you could drown. Hopefully all goes well, your parachute had collapsed one side and detached from your shoulder, you hit the water and you pull the toggle with the chord attached at the bottom of your PLP which inflates your life jacket. The indicator light will then activate showing the recovery team who are driving about in the water in rubber boats in your location and you get picked up. These boats are already in the water and they have been launched when your approach was indicated by radar as everything is on radio silence.

We were on the ground, scrounged kit and weapons—not good. And to top it all, the British Army had not been issued waterproof kits: no Gore-Tex, no waterproof boots. We were back in the First and Second World War situation—trench foot.

There is no doubt about it that the Falklands War was won by the high standard of training that all the units had. It was the men, not the equipment. Things have now changed in the British forces from lessons learnt in the Falklands and other conflicts. They now have access to some of the best equipment ever.

The world saw the war on television. You know what happened. It's on the Discovery Channel most days. You saw the homecoming and celebrations, but you didn't see the casualties we are still talking about, the mental problems still being suffered by the now not-so-young men who fought in that war.

I served the rest of my army career in the SAS, where I would go round the world training specialist units in the art of counter terrorism, it seemed like every country wanted a counter terrorist team like the UK had, they had all seen the Iranian Embassy on the television and what was achieved. I think I have been to most parts of the world more than once, lived in jungles, deserts and artic waste lands for months on end learning how to live, fight and survive in these climates and also train others from the British army and foreign forces to do the same. I am proud of my military career, I wouldn't have missed it for the world, it has made me into a determined, achiever who has learned not to give up regardless of the situation and that is one of the key points that I am trying to portray in this book. You can achieve the practically unachievable by determination and most of all the will to win. Have confidence in yourself and you will get through any situation.

When the time came to move on, I worked on what we call the circuit; this means jobs for ex-military people—some high risk, some not, depending on the job. I was offered a job in Sri Lanka training the police, who were in conflict with the Tamil Tigers. I turned this opportunity down to take on a job in London working for the owner of Harrods, Mr Mohamed Al Fayed.

In this photograph Bob is wearing a DPM uniform and regimental beret with the famous winged dagger cap badge, proudly earned. He is teaching foreign special forces how to strip and assemble a German H & K MP5 submachine gun. Notice the parachute harnesses hanging up in the rear.

Bob's flair for training was noted by his superiors, leading him to get plenty of training work all around the world, passing on his specialist skills learnt while serving in the regiment.

Always training out in the Middle East. You can see Bob firing an SLR 7.62 rifle. This is a favourite calibre for this environment, as you have greater range and harder impact against protected locations—hence better penetration, especially against soft-skin vehicles and lightly constructed defensive positions. A very reliable weapon, but quite heavy to carry, and so is the ammunition. This rifle was semiautomatic, hence only single-shot. However, there was also available the FN rifle, which had very similar characteristics and selective fire, hence fully automatic. Special forces need a variety of weapons at their disposal to suit the various terrains they operate in.

Here you can see Bob shooting a GPMG with a belt of two hundred rounds on it. Every fifth round is a tracer to indicate the strike. This may look like a 'gung-ho' way to shoot this weapon, but it was perfectly normal in built-up areas and when assaulting positions where enemies were dug in or in buildings. Notice the strap on the shoulder, which takes the weight of the weapon and gives the firer more control, especially with the butt of the gun tucked into the hip. Once again demonstrating the need to train for different situations.

20

THE AL FAYED FAMILY

I worked for the Al Fayed family for three years. My first year was with Dodi Fayed as his personal BG (bodyguard). I had been trained in the SAS to do this job and had taught others whilst in the military. I went to many places with him, including all the best clubs in London, and met many stars of the movies and music industry. He was a popular person and had a lot of friends. I got on very well with him. He would ask me about the SAS, as he had spent some time at Sandhurst as an officer cadet. I remember him asking me one day if SAS selection was as hard as Sandhurst. I said, 'Almost, sir.' He had a boat in St Tropez, and I would go there with him. There were film stars present on many occasions. It was a charmed life. All I had to do was look after him, which I did.

One of his closest friends was Barbara Broccoli, the daughter of Chubby Broccoli, who made all the Bond films. I got on very well with her. She would always acknowledge me when we met with a hug and a kiss on the cheek. Dodi would look at me, not impressed.

Dodi would go to America quite often on Concorde. I asked if I could go with him. He said he would love to take me, but unfortunately the people he used out there were policemen who were allowed to work in protection duties and get paid even though they were not doing their police shifts. They had badges and guns; that was enough.

One day Dodi's father asked about me and how I was doing with his son, because there hadn't been any trouble anywhere—not that he would have expected it. He was told by the person who ran his security that he was being looked after very well and that I was very capable, and that he was lucky to have found me. This wasn't a good thing. His father said, 'If he's that good, then I want him with me.' I was taken away from Dodi and put in charge of one of his father's close protection teams as a team leader.

We flew around the world in his private jet and private helicopter. I had to make sure that everything worked, that men were where they were supposed to be, and that luggage was there. I checked aircraft for any surprises that someone might have left for us. We searched everything. It had to be right.

We would take the whole family and all the nannies on holiday. I had to be alert all the time. It was down to me if anything went wrong. It never did. I was never going to let it. I fell back on my training every day. I had a good team working with me: ex-paras, marines, and military policemen. You have to have good men around you if you want to be successful.

Even though I was running this team, I missed working with Dodi. He'd appreciated me, as he'd known what he had working with him. I had worked with him on a week-on, week-off basis, and when I had not been there, another person would take over. He used to ask me why other people didn't open his car door for him and put him in the car, or why they let him walk through doors first or stand at the back of the lift instead of at the front by the doors. I said, 'Well, sir, they haven't had the same training as I have.' This was unfortunate, because not everybody that did the job was BG-trained at that time.

What is the job? Well, it's not punching people or rolling around on the floor with someone. It's seeing a situation as it develops and reacting by removing your subject from harm's way as quickly as possible using body protection—your body.

The job also entails always maintaining your subject's public image. You're with him because he is either rich or famous, and he doesn't want his reputation ruined by an incident that could be embarrassing to him.

Even though it was a glamorous life, I wanted to do something for myself, so I moved on. I decided to go into business for myself. One skill I had been taught in the SAS was lock entry, so I started looking into the possibility of my own locksmith business and training school, because there is always money in training. I had been trained to do lock entry to a high standard in the military, and it was obvious that civilian locksmiths did not have the same level of skill, so there was an opening, if you like, for a good training school. So I started my own.

It was with great sadness, years later, that I heard about the death of Dodi Fayed and Her Royal Highness Diana, the Princess of Wales. I had met the princess on many occasions. She came to Hereford to spend a day with the SAS the day before Diana and Prince Charles flew to Australia. I was on the counterterrorist team at the time, so they came to us for some fun. I always remember her fondly. She was a lovely-looking lady, ever so polite. She couldn't do enough for you and was genuinely interested in what you did and who you were. This country lost a wonderful person that day, along with my friend Dodi Fayed, who I know would have progressed in the film industry and made a great name for himself, as he did with his film *Chariots of Fire*, which I know he was extremely proud of. These two lovely people are sadly missed by this country, and I know their families miss them too, so I send to them love and light.

A year or so later I was approached by an author who, as he put it to me, wanted to know where all the skeletons were buried. By this he meant he wanted 'dirt' on the family. He was asking me because he knew that I had worked for them.

Well, there is a thing called loyalty. I had worked for them for a few years, and what I saw and did stayed private. This journalist was asking me questions that could damage reputations. I didn't believe what he was saying and quite honestly had been dreamed up by someone with a wild imagination clearly trying to discredit the family and individual members. I had an interview with this person for an hour or so and told him nothing that wasn't already in the public domain. He wanted me to get others who had worked there at the time to meet with him and give their stories, once again looking for dirt.

I said before that loyalty is something that is lacking in this world. People do anything for money, no matter what it would do to others, so I telephoned the head of security for the Al Fayed family and explained I'd been approached and that requests had been made for information, and that I wasn't prepared to discuss this with others—therefore, could an interview with Mr Al Fayed be arranged the following day? I received a call to come to London.

I arrived in London on the day and the time requested. I met with the head of security, who wanted me to hand over the request to him. I said no. A telephone call was made and I was escorted to Mr Al Fayed's office. He looked pleased to see me and had his usual smile. We shook hands. Present was one of his advisers. I said to him that this was serious and I didn't feel that anyone else should be present. The others left, and I handed him the typed minutes of the meeting and the list of requests.

He said as he read through it, stopping to laugh at certain parts, 'Yes, I know where this has come from. These people are trying to harm my reputation.'

I said, 'Yes, I know. That's why I'm here.' He was most grateful for my loyalty and thanked me with a smile.

It was agreed that we would speak to his legal team and that I would make a statement to them of what had been requested. This was arranged in minutes, as their office was just around the corner. I arrived there and explained what had happened. They knew who was behind this. It was quite obvious that all of this had been done for money, but many things are these days, and knowing what I knew, none of it was true.

It was agreed that a meeting would be set up with this journalist, and he would be misled all over the country whilst everything he said would be recorded as an admission on his behalf. He would be asked why he believed these things he told us. All this would be recorded.

People think they can go around throwing dirt at others. Well, that's not good. After several months, this eventually came to an end—the end that we wanted, not that he wanted. We made him work for what he wanted and he never got it.

The book was published, and there on the front page was my name. He wasn't happy. He tried very hard to discredit me in the book, but once again it was fiction despite everything that had happened he still wrote in his book

21

WHY DID I COME INTO MEDIUMSHIP?

As I explained previously, a road accident that I was involved in back in 1996 opened up my mediumship capabilities. This was also after the death of a very good friend, at his own hand. Afterwards I went along to a demonstration of mediumship by the very gifted Tony Stockwell, a world-renowned medium, at Chrickhowell, Wales. I had never seen a medium work before and didn't really know what to expect.

I knew they gave people readings, but to what extent and what was involved was a mystery to me. Tony was appearing at an old-world hotel perfect for this type of thing. When you walked in, the decor was all oak beams and panels. This took you back to the days when people rode horses and carried swords. To the right-hand side of the hall was a bar, where most people were going, and then upstairs was the demonstration of mediumship.

The room was filled with round tables with white tablecloths. In the centre of each table was a small white bowl of flowers. Everyone was taking a seat. There was no particular placing—just sit where you want. I sat at the back, out of the way, so I could see everything and watch the reaction on people's faces when they got a reading.

Tony arrived. There was a keyboard player in the corner, who I understand always travelled to these events with Tony. In front of the keyboard was a microphone, which he went up to and used to introduce himself to everyone, talking for a while about all sorts of things, but nothing to do with mediumship, which it's said he always did, so that he could get the feel of the room and those present and link with the spirit world.

Then, suddenly, he started giving a reading, explaining that he had someone with him and what the person looked like and who he thought the person was, and where he thought the recipient was sitting. This person was given a reading, and then he went on to another one. He did four in all and then declared a break. He left the room.

Everyone went down to the bar. Some thirty minutes later we were all seated and waiting for the second half of the evening. Tony came back behind the microphone and talked for a while, and then suddenly he looked at me and said, 'I have a young man here who took his own life. He is in his thirties, has a short haircut, and is wearing camouflaged clothes. He has a goatee beard and he keeps running it through his hands.' Tony said. 'I think he's a bit of a perv. He's got his bits out in front of me.' And then he pointed at me and said 'Do you know this person?', '

Then a microphone was handed to me, and Tony asked if I knew him. 'Yes,' I said. 'Very well, and you're right, he was a bit of a perv.' He went on to describe Martin. I was amazed at the accuracy of the information he gave me, and what I found very strange was that all the time Tony was talking to me, it was like I was looking down a tube at him. I don't know if you have ever looked down an empty toilet roll. It was the same—just like a tunnel.

This was fantastic. How could he do that? It was amazing. At the end of the evening I went to see Tony and explained how accurate he was and how Martin had committed suicide. He said, 'Yes, I know. I saw it.' I don't know what it was. There was something about Tony I was drawn to. It was like an energy I felt, like I knew him, but we'd never met before. I felt completely at ease with him. This was a magical moment, and any of you that have been in this situation would know what I mean. It's hard to describe.

I saw Tony three more times around the country. What a gift. But what I did not know, or was not aware of, was that I could do the same as Tony— well, probably not as good at the time, but that's going back a few years, and the fact that I can do it has been a great achievement for me. I'm not saying for one moment that I'm as good as Tony Stockwell, but in his own words, I 'have a very good link with Spirit,' and coming from him, that's good enough for me.

I don't want to sound bigheaded. I just love doing what I do. It's a fantastic feeling when I give information to the recipient and I am 100 per cent accurate. This proves beyond doubt that the link to the spirit world is there and connected. I have helped so many people with their lives. I would meet Tony again, many times, and eventually study Spiritualism and the art of mediumship with him as my mentor.

I moved from where I was living in the city to a village only about six miles away, for peace and quiet, as it was getting too noisy where I was and I felt a bungalow was the answer. The problem is that most older bungalows have been owned by elderly people who have passed to Spirit. This I was soon to find out.

It was September of 1999. I put my house on the market, and luckily enough, a man turned up to look at it. He wanted to buy it as an investment to rent. This was a three-bedroom end terrace built in the 1980s, so fairly modern, and of course in tip-top condition inside and out. House prices at the time were not doing well, so I was lucky to sell it, but I did.

The bungalow also had three bedrooms: one small bedroom at the front, a hall, a kitchen to the left, a living room to the right, another part of the hall, a bathroom to the left, and a bedroom to the right; the main bedroom, in the middle of those two, needed lots of work. We got it for a song, and as they say, if it looks too good to be true, it is.

We couldn't move in straightaway, as it needed new central heating and decorating from top to bottom. Some of the wiring required looking at, and it had a coal fire with a back boiler, which I had taken out and replaced with a log burner with glass front doors. This involved staying with relatives while this work was being done. I'm not a keen lover of other people's houses. I like my own space and the freedom that comes with it. Even to this day, if I visit anyone I will always stay in paid accommodation. It's just me. I don't like putting on people.

We had the whole bungalow painted magnolia. Some of the walls were bad and needed lining. We had trouble getting a decorator who could do it all at once without running off and doing three other jobs at the same time. We found one who lived in Bristol. He said it would be impractical for him to travel each day, so he asked me if he could stay in the bungalow and put an air bed on the floor. I saw no problem with this and said he was welcome to do it, thinking maybe he'd put more hours in and the get the job done.

So he stayed in the bungalow. He brought with him a camp bed. The shower worked. He was happy until I went to see his progress. Then he told me he felt that he was not alone in the bungalow. There was noise at night—doors opening and closing, footsteps. He looked scared. He only lasted a few days, then said he was ill and couldn't finish the job, and that I would have to find someone else. So he left.

Had he seen something? He never said, but I think so. Something had scared him. I had to get another decorator, and I was lucky. Someone I knew was on two weeks' holiday from work, intending to do his garden and put his feet up; however, cash waved under his nose changed his mind. He carried on where the other one had left off. His work was much better. I wish I'd had him in the first place.

Eventually the decorating was done, the plumbing was installed, and we moved in. Any of you who've moved house recently know the stress that is involved. It is not something I would do if I didn't have to. You just don't realise how many unwanted belongings you have, though they are always hard to part with, but you know you must. Charity shops always benefit from house moves, this I know.

So we progressed to building a home. However, it wasn't long before I noticed movement across the hall out of the corner of my eye. What was that? I investigated, but there was nothing there. But there was! This kept happening. It was obvious we were not alone. There was a spirit person in the bungalow.

I also noticed on several occasions a black cat darting past me. Only one problem—we didn't have a black cat. You could never find it when you searched the area. It disappeared, so it was clear this was a spirit cat. I'm sure you've seen them before. You think, *What was that?* Yes, it was a spirit cat.

I said nothing to my partner about this, as I was unsure of the reaction, but what I did not know was that she had seen it as well. This I discovered when I came home late one night and all the lights were on. So it all came out. She had known for a while but said nothing. Something had to be done, or we were possibly on the move again, because I know that she was concerned about this presence, and as she is not psychic, I think it frightened her.

My partner was speaking to a friend who knew of somebody who had a similar situation in her home, and she was told that this person had contacted a Spiritual church to have a clearing. This apparently involved church members coming to the house and carrying out a clearing to try and get the spirit person to move on. So we did this. We contacted the same Spiritual church. It was arranged for them to come around one evening. I asked how much the fee would be to do the clearing and was told to just give a donation to the church.

The night arrived, and a man and a lady arrived at the time arranged. I just did not know what to expect. A candle was lit and they walked around the rooms with sage tied up in a small handheld bunch that resembled a broomstick. 'Ah, I've found it. It's in the bathroom,' the man said. *Oh good*, I thought. *Now maybe it will go away and leave us alone.*

'It's gone,' the man said. 'You'll be okay now.'

'Great,' I said. 'Shall we have a cup of tea to celebrate?' We did, but it would be too soon. While the tea was getting ready, I talked about their work and the Spiritual church that they came from. It was all very interesting, especially when they said that they had a medium on every Sunday. I had to know more. I talked about the things that had happened in my life and the spiritual things that I had seen. They were very interested, and it was suggested that we come to church on Sunday to see for ourselves. However, it was pointed out to me that I would not be popular, as I see things and the average medium does not. It wouldn't be long before this would be proven true.

Sunday came around and we attended the church. There were about thirty people there, a good turnout by all accounts. We were made welcome and given tea, and at ten thirty the service began. There was a guest medium who conducted most of the service, and at eleven it was time for the medium to do his thing. He started giving a message to one of the audience, and I was getting some of the message myself. It was like I could carry on the reading on my own.

As I sat there and looked around, I started seeing people that were not there and seeing situations happening like a film running in front of me. This was all new to me. I now know that it was the energy in the room, the spirit people trying to get through. I could have stood up and given many readings, and this was my first time in church.

After the service I was asked what I thought of the service. Well, when I said what had happened, I was looked at like, *Yes, well of course you did.*

I was warned that this would happen. People don't like others with a natural gift, especially when they are trying and struggling with it themselves. I relate it to an Olympic athlete and others struggling to achieve the same standard; this is very hard work, but there is a very big natural ability there—not just anyone can do it to that standard.

Not suggesting I'm Olympic standard, but I do know that I have a natural gift that comes easier to me than to many others, and I am also aware that this has upset a few other mediums on the way. I attended this church every Sunday, as I wanted to get into mediumship. I just knew I could do it.

Eventually I would conduct the service myself and give readings on a regular basis, and also write poems for the church, which I never knew I could do. I found it all fairly easy. I was used to talking to people, all my readings are spirit guided, I would not do this any other way. This I'm proud of.

22

THE LEARNING CIRCLE

I was told that a leaning circle was the answer, but how did I find one? One Sunday a female medium took the service. I was talking to her afterwards, and I said that I was looking for a learning circle. She said I was in luck and that she would be starting one soon, and I would be welcome. I went along.

I did not know what to expect or what would happen. It was mostly ladies who attended, but there were two other men. Circles seem to be very female-oriented, for some reason, and I find that there are quite a number of gay men who attend as well. It must be the sensitive side of them that helps. I don't have a problem with anyone, no matter what their preference. I get on with them all, and some of the nicest people that I have ever met have been gay.

Anyway, we started with meditation. This is without doubt one of the best ways to get good links with Spirit. We would all sit in a circle of chairs looking inwards, and the lights were dimmed. We would close our eyes and be talked through a journey by the medium. I will explain what I mean by 'journey':

You are all going through a door, down some stairs into a garden. You can feel the sun on you. It's warm. You can smell the flowers in the garden. You have no shoes on, so you can feel the grass under your feet. You walk slowly through the garden on a sandy path to a beach. You walk along the sand. You can feel it between your toes. You hear the sea crashing on the shore. You smell the sea. You hear the seagulls. You paddle in the sea and notice a dolphin coming towards you. You wade out to it and hold on to its dorsal fin. It takes you down under the water. You can breathe. It's okay. It takes you down, down. You see a city at the bottom of the sea. It takes you through the streets. You see the people. You go on, and there in front of you is a cave. You go in. You see a book lying on a table. It's gold and it's closed. You read the writing on the front cover. What does it tell you? You open the book. What does it say?

You leave the cave, holding on to the dolphin back through the town, up, up to the surface of the sea, back to the seashore. You watch the dolphin swim away down into the sea. You walk up the beach, back to the house, through the garden, and up the steps to the door, through the door, up the stairs, and back into the room.

And then the medium will say to come back into the room, and you open your eyes slowly. You all talk about your experience, what you saw and what it said on the book cover and what you read in it.

This would take the first hour of the learning circle sitting. Then you would go on to do some psychic learning work. It might be working with energies. One member of the group might sit in a chair in the middle of the circle and close his or her eyes or be blindfolded, and everyone will get up and walk around the circle of chairs, just like Pass the Parcel, then be told to stop, and one person will then go and stand behind the one sitting in the chair.

Then the medium running the circle says, 'Is it a male or female standing behind you?' The person sitting on the chair answers, but it won't be confirmed whether the person is male or female. And then the medium asks, 'What colour do you feel?' An answer is given—say, 'red.' Maybe the person behind has a red top on, or the player may well be wrong.

The height of the person, the hair—long or short—etc., will all be asked, and then the final question: 'Who do you think it is?' An answer is given, and the person sitting down is asked to turn around to see who it is; sometimes he or she is right, and sometimes not.

Ribbons can also be used to get the energy of others. A bag containing coloured ribbons is handed around. Each person takes one without showing it to the others. Then, holding the ribbon in both hands, everyone rubs their hands together, putting their energy into the ribbon. Then the bag is handed around again for all to put in their ribbons. When all the ribbons are back in the bag, it's handed around for each to take one out and tell the group about the person he or she thinks it was handled by. Then the person who put their energy in the ribbon is asked to speak up. This will show if the reading was right or wrong.

I found all this interesting and very easy to do. I just seemed to have a flair for it. I wanted more. I could stand up and give messages. My one-to-one readings were spot-on. I needed more.

One Sunday I was talking to one of the people that run the church about the circle and the fact that I wanted to progress faster, as I felt that I could do the work fairly quickly. Well, in a phone call that evening it would all change. The same person from the church rang me and told me that I needed to go to Stansted Hall at the renowned Arthur Findlay College. It's the leading Spiritualist college in the world, so the next day I was on the Internet looking for this college. There it was.

23

SPIRITUALISM – THE RELIGION

Spiritualism is a religion that is growing in interest. People are understanding that there is something in it. It is the only religion that gives evidence of survival after passing. Other churches rely on the Bible as evidence, which is fine if there has been no distortion over the years from the original document.

Spiritualism puts you in touch with loved ones that have actually walked the earth plane. These relatives can be communicated with; they can be asked questions and can show the medium situations that happened in the past that couldn't possibly be known without assistance from someone that was actually there—hence the spirit person.

I know for a fact that Spiritualism is not understood by other churches, as I've got personal experience from speaking to vicars and clergy who have just smiled when I mention it. They don't seem to understand or believe what we say is actually realistic. As far as they are concerned, in my experience, they deny that spirit people exist and are of the opinion that once you've passed, you've passed.

However, I know that this is not true. As I said before, I have actually seen spirit people and communicated with them and still do on a daily basis, and they certainly do exist. It is a fact that when we pass to the spirit world, we don't disappear forever; we are around. We know what's going on. We can help in situations on the earth plane—not by interference, but by prompting in certain circumstances.

I'm sure you will agree that you have all been in a situation where you think, *Should I or shouldn't I?* You are unable to make your own mind up. There is the true saying, 'Go with your heart.'

And I'm sure that many of you who went with your heart found it was the correct direction. I feel that going with the heart is a form of communication with the spirit world. Spirits can indicate to you the path that you should take, you should listen to Spirit as they are trying to direct you. I have been in many situations where I have gone with my heart and found it to be the right direction. It is also a fact that any situation you find yourself in will correct itself in time.

Whether this situation is debt, the loss of employment, poor housing, or a relationship that has gone badly wrong, many people in such circumstances have taken their own lives. This is not the answer. Just think about who you will leave behind: partners, husbands, wives, children. All of these have to live with the fact that you took your own life. Could they have done something to prevent this? They blame themselves and feel that if they had only just come to me, I could have helped. 'How can people do this?' they ask me. 'Did they feel that I couldn't be trusted?' As any one of you will know who has been in this situation knows that the incident stays with you for life. Always talk to people; there are ways out of anything.

No matter what it is, there is light at the end of the tunnel, and light is so important to us. It is a continuation of the soul. It goes on. We all need light. The spirit world would not be pleased with us if we consider committing suicide, as it is not our time to pass back to the spirit world. Our earth plane journey is not complete. We still have more to learn.

People that commit suicide cause sorrow for their loved ones and people that knew them. They leave them with guilt. And what about the poor soul who finds your body? How do you think he or she feels? t affects all. There is a saying, 'It's good to talk.' I strongly believe in this, and so should you.

I'm not condemning other religions, as everyone believes in their own god, and this keeps us on the straight and narrow. Everyone has to have rules to live life by, or else what would we have, anarchy? But going back through the ages, how many people have talked about seeing ghosts? Many. You see this situation in films all the time. They even make science fiction films about it. We should also consider the popularity of the paranormal programmes that we see on television on a regular basis, where people go out and actively look for so-called ghosts. They are actually hunting spirit people. Why? Because they are there.

I feel that this proves on its own what I am saying. Unfortunately, there are certain presenters and television personalities who have involved themselves with paranormal activities, these activities just to make good television. And when something does happen or they create something in their own minds, they fall apart, start screaming, and run away. Why?

Because they weren't looking for the spirit person in the first place, and when they found him or her, all they could do was panic and run off.

If genuine mediums did this every time they encountered a spirit person or communication from a communicator, where would we be? No one would ever get the message. Pandemonium would rule, and there would be no such thing as Spiritual churches.

I've been on many occasions to churches of all religions, for weddings, christenings, etc., and have seen spirit people present in these churches. I was at a wedding and the church walls were covered in wood panelling, and as I was admiring it, I looked to the right of the altar and noticed a monk standing there with his hood up and his hands interlocked up his sleeves.

This monk stood there for most of the service, clearly watching the proceedings. It was obvious that he had been there at that church as a working monk, and his presence was clearly visible to anyone who had clairvoyant ability.

The question many people ask is why are these people still here? Some will tell you that they are grounded, having unfinished business to attend to, worried about loved ones who are still on the earth plane, worried about situations that weren't resolved before they passed. A lot of people will tell you, as I said, that they are grounded and need to pass to the spirit world.

Do we really know the answer? Is there anyone on the earth plane that can answer this question? I've asked many knowledgeable people who have been involved in mediumship for many years, and I get different answers. No one seems to agree on what is actually happening or going on, but one thing is for sure: these are people, and when I say 'people,' I mean they were people when they were on the earth plane.

So why should that change just because they've passed? I don't see the difference. They are still your loved ones. You still love them the same, and I think it is nice of them to come and visit you, even though it might be the biggest shock of your life. I'm sure it is a big effort to materialise in front of you so that they can be recognised.

I was talking one day with another medium when this actually happened in front of our eyes. I can only relate this to what is seen on *Star Trek*, the science fiction programme on the television, when someone gets in the glass tube and forms into sparkling dust and either disappears or appears. This is exactly what happened right in front of our very eyes. However, whoever it was trying to communicate with us was unsuccessful. I found this totally fascinating and wish they could have formed in front of me. I wouldn't have run screaming; I would have been very pleased to see them, and so would the other medium.

Just imagine if our relatives could come back in this form and visit us. Wouldn't it be wonderful? I've seen this in many communications, with the communicator at an age far younger than that at which they passed. It is said that when we pass we revert back to the age at which we were happiest on the earth plane. This was proved to me recently when I was at the Arthur Findlay College, and a psychic artist was drawing a picture of a communication with a spirit person as another medium stood there doing the communication.

The communicator was in fact my father, who had passed to the spirit world only a few years before. There is no way that the psychic artist could have possibly known what my father looked like, and the fact that he had passed wasn't written on any form or mentioned in any overheard conversation. However, she was able to do an extremely good likeness of him, and as I was saying, he appeared many years younger than when he'd passed, which to me proves this theory beyond doubt: we definitely revert back to the age we were happiest whilst on the earth plane.

I recently read the eulogy at a funeral, and I had to meet with the vicar who was conducting the service some days before the actual event. When I mentioned Spiritualism I got a polite smile from him. It was clear he didn't believe in it whatsoever. At the end of my speech on the day of the funeral, I referred to the person who had passed by saying that he or she had in fact gone to the spirit world, and I wished him or her love and light.

The vicar sat to one side watching the proceedings, and when I said those words, once again he gave a polite smile. It was clear he didn't believe a word of it. However, to each his own. He's not wrong. Neither am I. The fact is the day went well, and it was a celebration of life and passing back to the spirit world.

I have been asked to speak at many funerals at the request of relatives of the person who has passed. On one occasion I was told that they didn't want someone standing there talking about their loved one and breaking down, which I don't seem to do, as it has never happened yet nor do I feel it will. To me a funeral is not a sad day of passing. This person has completed his or her task on the earth plane and is merely going back to the spirit world, where without question we will all meet again.

24

MALARIA WAS BACK

I suffered with malaria, which I had contracted in a jungle somewhere around the world, for several years after leaving the army. It would hit me hard and I would break into the worst sweat. I would feel cold and my body would shake. One time I had it so bad that I had to go to bed; I was bad. I got into a sleeping bag and under a duvet but still felt freezing cold, shaking, and delirious.

Then it happened. I was in this state of illness, soaking wet in the sleeping bag, when I saw a bright light. And it was *bright*—like looking into a car headlight full-on at close range. I was walking down a tunnel towards the light, the bright light. I was near the end when I was stopped. The end had bars in square shapes across it. I was pulled back fast. Then I woke up and sat up in bed with not a care in the world; nothing mattered—no worries. What a feeling. I had been to the light and come back.

You will hear many people talk about this experience, about going to the light for various reasons. It could be a bad car accident. In near death situations where a person is either seriously injured in some way or has a bad illness and they survive you will hear them talk about going to the light, the tunnel of light. I feel qualified to speak about this. As I've mentioned above, I have been down the tunnel. I have had that experience and know what it's like. However, it wasn't my time. I still had work to do on the earth plane and was brought back out of the tunnel, away from the light, the crossover point to the spirit world.

People talk about out-of-body experiences wherein they are above situations happening around them, looking down on them—operations in a hospital where they are the patients, or accidents where they are the victims. They see what is going on. This is achieved by our soul looking down on our earthly body. This doesn't mean that we are crossing over to the other world; it just means that our soul came out of our body to review what was happening to us. I've also heard of situations wherein people have claimed they have seen the soul leave the body on passing.

Remember, your body is only your earth vehicle. What problems you have down here on the earth plane will be rectified when you return to the spirit world, so don't worry about passing; you are merely returning to where you came from, the spirit world.

There is a lot of sadness in this world of ours, as I hear during my one-to-one readings. We seem to be obsessed with greed and possessions. Marriages go on the rocks mainly due to people getting married too young and then wanting their lives back. Spouses feel caught in a trap. Then it's taken out on the children, or money always seems to be an issue in partnerships. What seemed to be a good idea at the time sometimes turns out not to be. These are earthly experiences we go through so that when we return to the spirit world, we will be much wiser.

I have been to every part of our world, and I must say that I find the happiest communities are those that have the least and live a simple life. Take the tribes in Brunei and surrounding areas: they have practically nothing. Their supermarket is around them in the trees. It's only a matter of walking a few yards to get food. Where we don't seem to have a minute, it's just rush around. We don't care about others. It's not our problem. They got into it, whatever the situation is, and even our children can't stand on their own two feet.

I now know that when spirits are about you often get a smell of tobacco or perfume, or sometimes a very bad smell. I have one in my home at present that brings a bad smell, and after several clearing attempts it's still there. I get a sighting of it from time to time. I see a man about in his eighties, small—by this I mean around five foot six—and he stands in the same place. Sometimes he will walk up to me and stand by me. I don't find it a problem. I know that some would.

Pets are also very good spirit detectors. They will stare at an area for a long time, looking very alert. Their heads may go from side to side, still staring in the same direction.

There have been a few encounters with Spirit in my life, It was in 1996 when my spiritual life changed. I was driving to Gloucester, I was on a dual carriageway approaching a roundabout. I looked to my right and saw a brown lorry coming around the roundabout, so I gave way to it as you are supposed to do. The next thing I knew was that I was being catapulted across the road. I had been impacted from behind by a brown Vectra with two mountain bikes on the back of it.

I was violently thrown forward, but my seat belt saved me from being thrown about in the car. The back of the seat I was sitting on was broken from the impact, so back I went. I lay there for a while and then tried to get up out of the car. I could not move. My neck felt like it had swollen up many times; it had.

My partner was in the car with me. She had dropped her seat back and was lying down. I said, 'Are you okay?' She looked bad, as if she were going to be sick. Anyway, I managed to get out of the car and found that we were in the middle of the road. The next thing I knew was this very loud person—I'll call her a 'lady' for this book, but I can assure you she was in need of behaviour lessons and manners—appeared.

'Look what your spare wheel on the back of your car has done to my car!'

'I had a four-wheel drive,' I said. 'What are you talking about? You drove into the back of me.'

'But you just stopped,' she said.

'Yes, because of the lorry coming round the roundabout.'

'What lorry?' she said. She hadn't even seen it or me.

I phoned the police to tell them that we were in the middle of the road, and they responded, for all the good it did. As soon as the police car arrived, she went straight up to the officer and said that I had just stopped, causing her to hit me, and I had jumped out on my mobile calling the police.

The police asked if we wanted to go to hospital, but my partner said she didn't. This would come back to haunt me, as Gloucester Hospital scans road accidents victims. Had I been scanned at the time, the extent of my injuries would have come to light.

Anyway, apparently this accident activated my psychic side, and this is when my visual sightings started.

25

POEMS

I was asked by a Spiritual church to write a poem about war for Remembrance Day, the eleventh day of the eleventh month. I had never written a poem before, but I'm always up for a challenge, and this is what I wrote.

Gallant Men

Gallant were the one hundred as they rode into the valley of death.
Gallant were the millions
who went off to do their best.
This war will be over by Christmas, the politicians were heard to say.
No worries, they thought, because we won't have to go anyway.
Gallant were the millions on both sides who died at the Somme, and gallant were the mutilated who had to live on.
Gallant were the men who escaped at Dunkirk, and the small boats that saved them.
It had to work.
Gallant were the men who landed on D-Day to stop the evil occupation,
but knew with their lives they may have to pay.
Gallant were the Forces as they went into Iraq to stop the evil tyrant
and give the people
their country back.
Gallant are the men who fight in the Afghan war, whose brief is to stop
the surge of terrorism from our shores.
Oh, why can't the politicians see indeed, war was never the answer to
individual greed?
Gallant were these millions of men over the centuries that fought, so
that we could have freedom, of a sort.

'Gallant' is a word that we seem to use too much.
Maybe 'love thy neighbour,' would be a better touch.

Everyone liked it, but someone made a comment to the effect of, 'that lovely poem Bob *allegedly* wrote himself.' As if I had copied it. Well, it's all my own work; I don't go to that church anymore.

I am aware that I am gifted with different psychic abilities, these being clairvoyance, clairsentience, and clairaudience, which means I see, sense, and hear Spirit. This is something that was pointed out to me when I first started out on the mediumship path, as I have said. Why? Because others would not like it; they can't do it, so why should I be able to? I found this out when I started to attend a learning circle. Some people had been practicing mediumship for twenty years and still could not stand up and give a message. It was clear that newcomers were not welcome, and particularly men.

But not to be deterred, I battled on. I found out very quickly that I had a flair for one-to-one readings. The more you do them, the better you become. What I mean by this is you get a better, clearer connection with Spirit and a better understanding of what Spirit is trying to show you.

This is achieved by symbols, for instance. If a spirit person is sending a recipient good luck, he or she will show me a lump of coal. Strength is represented by a horse, calmness by water, etc. When you learn the symbols, it makes readings quicker for the people receiving them. Communicators often show me graveyards, telling me where they are and the fact that they were buried. Sometimes they still show me a graveyard even when they were cremated. I point this out to the recipient and I tell him or her that I'm being shown a graveyard where the communicator is buried. They often say no. My answer to this is that the communicator's ashes must be there; this is why I'm shown it. The recipient answers yes.

Recently I did a reading for a lady who I saw had two sons. One was bright and outgoing and had an interest in music; the other was dark and lay in bed or on the settee in the living room. She said yes, but when I linked with him all I could see was darkness. I said to her, 'It's as if I'm in a ball, a black ball.' She said yes, there was a reason for that. It would not come. All I could see was darkness. I kept asking Spirit to show me why, although all it showed me was darkness. I said to the recipient, 'I'm sorry. All I'm getting is darkness. I know this doesn't feel good. I know something is wrong.'

She said, 'Yes, there is a reason for this. He's dead.' She then asked me, 'Can you get him through for me?' I said I would try and link with him in the spirit world. This is something that I've always been able to do since the start of my mediumship capabilities. I went into deep thought and communication, asking Spirit to bring him to me, link us up, and let me see him so I could describe him to his mother and explain what I was getting from them.

And then I said to her that he had dark hair. She said yes. I also told her that he had a smile that you couldn't mistake, which was very noticeable about him. She said, 'Yes, you got him.' I also saw problems with the way he had been living on the earth plane and the situation in which he had passed back to the spirit world. I said this to his mother and she agreed. I knew this because I had him with me. What people need in this situation is hard evidence that you have their loved one with you, and as a medium you have to produce this for them—something you couldn't have possibly known, something only the mother, in this case, would know.

I told her he was showing me a football, a small football. It was a trophy, and there as a footballer with his foot on the trophy. It was in gold, and the ball was black and white. She said, 'Yes, we have that trophy in his father's bedroom.' I also said to her that he was showing me a green army tank. I didn't know why. She said, 'Yes, I know. It was a robot that he had that you could turn into different objects, and one was a green army tank. His favourite toy.'

At this stage the tears were coming in. I said to her, 'He gives you a large white bunch of flowers.' He was standing there with his hand out with the flowers in them. I said, 'Would you recognise these flowers?'

She said, 'Yes, they are lilies, my favourite.' At this stage, I must admit, I was feeling emotional, as you have as a medium the feelings that come from the spirit world to the recipient through you. We ended the reading on a very good note.

$\mathcal{26}$

SPIRITUAL AND PSYCHIC READINGS

The Spiritual Reading

Mediums use different words to explain what they are telling you. This is achieved by the following.

Messages from the spirit world are from a person who has passed—by this I mean left the earth plane and gone to the spirit world. This person is the communicator, and you are the recipient, the person receiving the message. Mediums have guides who work as go-betweens for the communicator and the recipient; these can be all sorts of different people. They are in Spirit themselves, and they assist with the communication process; they are also there to keep any unwanted spirits that might cause harm or problems away from the medium.

We all have spirit guides. You know when they are working with you, and I know you have all been in situations where you asked yourself, *Should I or shouldn't I?* This is your spirit guide telling you to think about what you are about to do, as it might not be best for you.

I get it when I'm driving a car in a country lane and I suddenly get the feeling to slow down, and I do, and yes, there, just around the corner, is a tractor cutting the hedgerows, with a car or lorry overtaking it on my side of the road. There would have been a big collision. I'm sure this has happened to you.

When mediums works to give you a message, they should describe the person that is trying to communicate with you by giving you a description. For example, a medium might tell you that she has a person who was sixty-five years old when he passed. This person had walking difficulties and was also a smoker, and he is telling the medium that he worked in a factory making cars. He passed with cancer after a period of illness. Then the medium should ask if you know this person; if not, the medium must give you more information about the communicator—possibly that she feels that this person was related to you, or that this person was your uncle. All this will help. I'm lucky, as I am often shown a clock with the time on it and told if it is light or dark outside, which allows me to say the time of passing and whether it was day or nighttime. This is all evidence to the recipients that I have their relative with me.

Mediums are normally shown symbols whose meanings they have to interpret. For instance, if I were shown a lump of coal, this would mean that the recipient will possibly have some luck in the near future; or, if a person is holding the coal and I can see a colliery wheel behind him, I know the communicator worked in a coal mine. If I am shown running water, like a stream, this means that there is a situation around the recipient that needs calming down, as water in streams is calming to watch.

It takes time to learn what these symbols mean. In fact, it takes years of reading people, but one thing a medium must never do is try to make something fit. With this I am referring to when the recipient might say something to the medium that could indicate he or she is on the right track, and the medium then tries to make it fit with what he or she is telling the recipient. This is bad practice but does happen.

The best way to avoid this is to not give the medium any information to build on. Then, whether what you receive is correct or not, you will know it is truthful. Symbols can change. Recently I was giving a reading and I saw farmland. I said I felt that this person was connected with farming. The answer was no. Then I was told Wales, so I said there was a Welsh connection. Here the answer was yes. The symbol I knew for farming now had a double meaning.

I very rarely see pets unless they are important to the reading for the communicator. For example, a person I was describing always had a cream and white spaniel with him. This was very good evidence to the recipient. I work with Spirit as much as possible, as I believe this is the true reading to give to somebody. I know that I personally get the best information directly from Spirit. I found that it doesn't always flow quickly. Sometimes a communicator will give me a name. The recipient will accept it, and I will ask the communicator for other information to confirm to my recipient that I have with me who I say I have. I was recently tested by a male who admitted he was a nonbeliever and said that I would be embarrassed at my lack of ability to describe the person and his life to him. In fact, he was very sure I would fail.

He came in for a one-to-one reading with his partner. I said to him, 'I have your grandfather here.'

'Okay. What does he look like?' came the reply. I described him. He said, 'Okay. What was his job?' And at the same time he said, 'You'll never get this one.'

However, I had a good link with Spirit, and Spirit showed me fish. I said, 'There is a fish connection here.'

He said, 'No. I knew you wouldn't get it.'

I said, 'But it shows me fish.'

His answer was, 'In fact, he ate a lot of it.' This was evidence. He then said again, 'Go on, then. What did he do?'

I was shown from the spirit world a train, and replied, 'There is a railway connection here.'

Well, that changed everything. 'Bang on,' was the reply. 'How did you do that?'

I said quite simply, 'Your granddad was standing next to me. He shows me and tells me. In fact, he showed me a pair of checked carpet slippers.'

The recipient said, 'I don't believe it. He was Scottish and was proud of the tartan, and had a much-loved pair of tartan carpet slippers he always wore.'

I rest my case, I thought to myself.

I spoke on the telephone to his partner on the following day and asked what he thought. She said that he wished he knew how I did that so that he could con people as well. With all the evidence I had given him, there was no way in this world that I could have done it any other way than with a spirit link. It just goes to prove that regardless of how hard you try, there will always be the person who disbelieves.

However, for the few that don't believe, I have thousands who do. Like I said before, Spiritualism is the only religion that gives evidence of survival after the earth plane. I'm often asked if I can bring a relative through, a specific relative, which I'm able to do on many occasions, proving beyond doubt that we have the ability to communicate with Spirit when we want to.

Families have problems and always will, and this was true for mine recently. My partner was in a bad place, and because of it she asked me one evening to give her a reading to try and get her dad through and see what he had to say. I said I would try, as you can never guarantee a result. However, I established my links with the spirit world and first of all got my partner's grandmother. I could see that her dad was also present. He was trying to come forward and speak to me. Eventually he managed to come forward, and I discussed the situation with him. He gave me some very good advice, which was passed on to the recipient, my partner. After the reading I said, 'How was that, exact good advice or what?' She told me that while I was doing the reading I'd had a white light all around my head and blue stars on my face and head, and that my facial features had been changing. My eyebrows had gone bushy. Her dad had bushy eyebrows.

It has been said before that my facial features change and that there is activity around me in the form of lights and shapes when I give readings.

This is good, as it proves that I have the spirit link to be seen by all—or maybe not all. I watched Tony Stockwell on platform once, and he had a gold light above him and brilliant white light to the rear. This was his aura, which, like mine, can be clearly seen on some occasions. I once had an aura picture taken with a special camera, and it showed all the different colours around me. You could pick out the spiritual side of me by the colour that was represented.

I once also had a perfect demonstration of facial changing when one of the tutors at the Arthur Findlay College gave a demonstration of trance mediumship. He took on the look—by this I mean the facial change—of Winston Churchill as well as his voice. This was absolutely brilliant. He talked about the world and what we've done with it. Knowing the tutor who did this, it would have been totally impossible for him to even copy the voice, let alone transform into the character, without the help of Spirit. So it shows how good a genuine medium can be when put to the test.

The Psychic Reading

This is achieved by mediums using their psychic ability to read people and tell them things about themselves by looking at them and assessing them by their age, clothes, and mannerisms. Some mediums respond to reactions of information passed to the person being read by watching the persons eyes to see their reactions. I can mentally see a film running and look into the life of the person and I also have the ability to look around their home without actually being there. I am able to tell people what they have in the house and where it is, even down to the colour of the kitchen floor. I am shown everything. People are amazed at what I tell them. *How can I know this?* Well, I do, and I enjoy what I do. It's a gift without a doubt.

I can tell them how many children they have and if they are married, if their house is a semi or detached, if the semi is on the left or right side, if there is a garage, if the house is tidy or not. I see their eating habits—junk or healthy, convenience or properly prepared.

One thing I do look at is their relationships with their partners. Good or bad, it will show, even if there are three people in the relationship, which is sometimes the case. I'm not there to judge. I make this clear. What they do is up to them, not me, and everything I see is confidential; nothing goes out of that room.

I'm asked on many occasions to contact a relative who has passed while doing a reading. I explain that this may take a while, but if they want to make contact, I will try to get that person. And I often do. How do I do this? Well, I look hard into the spirit world and ask the relative to come forward and make contact with me—and there, suddenly, I often see a person coming into focus. Young or old, male or female, the person is there.

I then describe the person I see to the recipient: whether it is male or female, how old, hair colour, clothes. I ask the relationship from the communicator, and he or she tells me what it is—for example, mother, father, son, etc.

At this stage the recipient often asks me to put a question to the communicator, usually with regards to a concern that he or she has, like worry over not being there when the communicator passed, or wondering if he or she is forgiven for an argument that caused them not to speak to each other for years. People carry through life these and many more concerns that need to be answered.

The cause of passing is good evidence, I have found: heart attack, road accident, cancer, a fall, drowning. All good evidence for the recipient, and of course so are special words that will mean something instantly.

27

THE ARTHUR FINDLAY COLLEGE

I phoned the college and explained that I was new to mediumship. I asked what course I could attend. I was told that I needed a mixed-levels course, which sounded good, so I paid over the phone for the next available course at mixed levels. Most courses are run on a Saturday-to-Saturday basis. The day arrived and I drove to Stansted Airport as instructed, followed the signs to the long-stay car park, and drove past it as instructed. The road went on back over the motorway. I turned left at the bridge and the hall was on the right, down a single-track road with lots of speed bumps, and there at the end was this magnificent country mansion. It was glorious.

I knew I had arrived. This was where I was going to progress. I had to book in at 1500 hours. I was lucky. I had my own room on the top floor—nothing posh, single bed with basin, mirror, small wardrobe, and clean towels. We were told to assemble at 1700 hours for a talk and to decide which groups we were going into. I noticed the energy; it was strange. I was feeling good about this place. It felt right.

At 1700 hours we were all in the main hall in the house, by the beautiful oak stairs. Very nice. There were eighty of us from all over the world. There were students from the American Midwest, Germany, Australia, Scandinavia, Italy, Southern Ireland, Northern Ireland, every part of the world, almost. This was good. We had a questionnaire to complete about our experience of Spiritualism. I wrote that I had only been practicing for a few weeks, which I felt was true, and that I did not want to be put in a group of experts and look stupid with my lack of knowledge.

We were told to look on the notice board for our groups and group room numbers, and told to be there at 1930 hours.

Tea was at 1800 hours in the restaurant. There was a big queue outside it, so you had to be on time. What a nice place. Lovely staff. It was hot plates served by the staff, and it was all there: good choices and lovely desserts, which I left alone. The last thing I wanted was to put on weight, but at 1830 hours on the dot the food was cleared away. All the trays were cleared. This was efficiency working at full speed. You could see that they had done all this before, many times, and they knew the drill.

I went to the board and looked for my name. I was in Angie Morris's group, in what was the dining room when the house was in family use. We all gathered in this splendid room. You could feel the history as you looked around. We had chairs in a half circle around a stage, and we introduced ourselves to one another, like you do. Then Angie came into the room. I did not know what she would look like—maybe all mystic, black hair and lots of jewellery, but no. There was this lovely, very good-looking lady with blond hair, quietly spoken and obviously very knowledgeable in this subject. I felt good about all of this. This was for me.

Our first lesson was on aura colours, which was interesting and new to me, looking at people and seeing their auras. By this I mean that everyone has an aura, even animals. It's the colour that is around you; actually, it can be several colours, and often is. A lot can be told about you by this: how spiritual you are, what mood you are in, etc. It works, and there are many in-depth books on the subject.

We were all very keen to learn this subject, and it was good for me, but I wanted to give messages. Well, the next day I would get my wish. We went on to discuss auras until 2100 hours, when Angie said that the bar was open and she would see us at nine thirty tomorrow, so off we went to the bar. This was a very nice, well-decorated room with an outside area for the smokers or for taking in the summer evening. I'd given up drinking years ago, so soft drinks were my thing, but we did have part of our group that liked Pimms o'clock. This was instigated by a very lovely, very nice lady called Tiffany Crosara, who has now become a very successful spiritual medium and has written a bestselling book on the subject that can be found on the Internet—a recommended read. We got on well in our group.

Breakfast, 0800 hours. I was up long before this, walking around the grounds. What a lovely, peaceful place. There was a tree in the middle of the rear grounds with seats around it, known as the tulip tree. I sat there for some time watching the sun rise over some other trees, thinking what a lovely place I had come to, when I noticed that there were rabbits playing out in the open, not afraid that a human was so close by. I was just marvelling at this when I noticed a squirrel coming towards me. I thought to myself, *He's going to see me soon, and he will be off.*

But no. He came right up to me and jumped up onto the bench that I was sitting on and sat there right beside me. There was no fear in him. He knew that I would not hurt him. I felt that this was a message from Spirit that I was in the right place to progress and be welcomed to the spirit world. The squirrel looked at me and around him for some time, then just went up the tree without a care in the world.

The choice of breakfast was full English or continental—loads of every-thing. I had a preference for filter coffee at the college. It was always there. We were to sit at the same table for every meal, which apparently helped the staff. By 0845 hours breakfast was gone, so if you were up late, it was tough—you missed your breakfast.

At 0930hours, it was all to the sanctuary. This was like a church for morn-ing thoughts and a sing-a-long. The person in charge was called Colin Bates—one of the nicest, funniest people you could wish to meet. What a star he is. I just found everything he said so funny. One mealtime he rang the bell that they had in the restaurant to get our attention, and said, 'I haven't got a message. I just wanted to ring the bell.' Well, you can imag-ine the response, but that was him.

A good sing-a-long was the order of the day to get you in high spirits for the day's work, and it worked: eighty people of all ages, from all over the world, singing 'I Had a Dream' by ABBA. What an experience. It could have been recorded and sold as a record from the college. Fantastic. The energy that this produced was beyond belief. You knew that you were part of something very good that was happening in front of your very eyes. An unbelievable experience. I've been to the college five times now and have never found energy like it elsewhere. I can't recommend it enough.

Anyway, we went to our groups, to our designated rooms, and in came Angie. 'We are going to do platform work today. This involves standing on a stage and giving messages to an audience. Who wants to go first?'

'Well, yes, I will,' I said, having seen this done before and feeling confident in talking. And as I spent my days teaching, anyway, I knew I could hold an audience.

I got up and looked around at everyone, who I'm sure expected me to clamp up with nothing to say, but no. I saw a girl of about ten years with a silvery grey bike by some railings, and I was shown a red lorry. I said, 'Can anyone take a girl of about ten who passed on a silvery grey bike by some railings? And a red lorry was involved.' And to my amazement the lady from Northern Ireland said, 'I can.'

I said, 'She is okay now. She can walk again, and her bike is fixed.' I knew this because the spirit girl was smiling at me in what I can only describe as a full-colour film running in front of me.
I could do it. I could pass messages just like Tony Stockwell and the mediums in the church. I was so pleased. I was not wasting my time and money at the college. Angie asked if I could do another one, and I did, and then stepped down to let someone else have a go.

A lady from Germany was asked if she would like to try. As she looked at me, she replied, 'He is like a teacher. I can't do that.' What she didn't know was that I was surprised that I could!

I went on to surprise myself many times. We did a lot of things on the course. Healing was new to me. I worked with another Angie in the group, who was from Norfolk. We got on very well. One day I was doing healing on her in the sanctuary as part of the group, noncontact—hands above the person that you are giving the healing to—when the tutor came over to us and said that she could see a bright golden light around both of us. It was amazing. I have since completed a Reiki course, but did not progress further due to the problems that it might bring with working with ladies and the lack of a female assistant. But I know that I can do healing and have had good results.

We went on to do many things on the course, all very interesting. We worked with colours and energies and had a brilliant demonstration of trance, the best that I have ever seen, by Colin Bates. He sat in a chair on the platform and went into a trance and became Winston Churchill. It was him. His face changed to that of Winston, and the voice was his as well. I have never seen anything like it to this day. It was mind-blowing. He was Winston Churchill right in front of our eyes.

It was quite a long speech, lots of warnings about looking after the earth and ourselves. At the end he just sat there for a while and had to be helped up. He sat at the back of the room with a drink of water. I have seen many attempts at trance over the years, but no one as good as Colin.

The days were long: 0930 hours to 2100 hours for seven days. That's hard work, but it was fun, and I learnt a lot about mediumship. I would come again to the college four more times, the third time on Tony Stockwell's week. Tony teaches there one or two weeks a year as a course organiser. I attended a week, not in his group but in the same course. It was my own fault that I was not in his group, as you have to grade yourself, and I didn't think I was that good, so the week I spent there was a bit of a waste, as I could have been in his group. Why did I want to be? Well, he is the master, brilliant. What better than to be an understudy of his?

This is the man that first showed me mediumship, back at Chrickhowell in Wales when he brought my friend Martin through—

The next year I booked Tony's course, and this time I would be in his group. The time came to attend Tony's course at 1500 hours, and the course was full, as it always was on Tony's week. There was a waiting list to get on it. At 1700 hours we were given the sheets asking us what level we thought we were. There were two levels at the top, Advanced Group and Teaching Group. Now, there was a problem: no tutor's name on any course. What was Tony teaching? It had to be one of the top two. Which would I choose?

I didn't want to do teaching, as I did that all day in my job, so I went for the advanced group. Spirit must have been with me that day, as when we got to our group rooms, I was in the large lounge. Tony walked in. 'Hi, group.' Yes, it was like *X Factor*, when they discover their mentors. Now I would learn.

There was an introductory chat. Names were given so he could remember us. He told us that we were going to divide into pairs, and he wanted us all to give the name of someone who had passed to the spirit world and tell each other all about that person. 'Bob, you can come and work with me,' he said. Well, can you imagine? Day one, lesson one, and there I am reading for the master.

He gave me a lady's name. 'Off you go,' he said. 'What can you tell me?'

I said, 'I see a bus. I have an age of about twenty-seven.'

'Yes,' he said.

'I see this lady, not tall, about five foot six inches.'

'Yes,' he said.

'I see an office block with tinted windows.'

'Yes,' he said.

'They keep showing me a bus,' I said.

'Yes.'

'This lady had a well-paid job.'

'Yes.'

'Now I'm up north between Newcastle and Scotland.'

'Which one?' he asked.

'Scotland.'

'Where?' he said.

And I said a place whose name I can't remember as I write this, but whatever it was, Tony said, 'Spot-on.'

He then went on to tell me that it was a lady he knew. The age that I'd given him was right. She had been on the way up in her profession, and she'd passed when a bus or coach was in collision with a car in the place in Scotland that I'd said.

'Very good,' he said to me. Well, how do you think I felt? I had just impressed the master. No doubt about it, I was now on the way, going up. I should have been in this group last time. I waited a year to do that. If you think you can, then go for it; that's my advice to you. Don't hold back.

It was a brilliant week with Tony. He confirmed lots to us. I asked his advice on small things that had happened in my one-to-one sessions, and I was surprised to learn that he had experienced some of the same situations in readings that I had.

Tony Stockwell has got to be the best medium that we have in this country at the present time. If you feel that you have the gift that I have been talking about and want to enhance it, this is the place to start, the Arthur Findlay College, Stansted.

The Arthur Findlay College is also the headquarters of the National Spiritualist Union, of which I am now a full member. Many of you out there who are mediums might wonder why I would bother to join this organisation. Well, all I can say, with respect, is it's all about bits of paper in life—that is, we have to prove to everyone that we can do what we say. Yes, you can be a brilliant medium and popular in your own area, but there are always those who doubt what you do. You don't get membership in the SNU without being tested by the best, and this to me was a proud achievement, like getting a degree at a top university that is well-respected worldwide.

Stansted Hall

I love Stansted Hall. It will help with my mediumship, so I can learn it all.
I study here all day. I don't need time to play.
I'm told I can learn a lot, but be careful you don't lose the plot

The people I meet there are very good, loving, and kind, and full of sister and brotherhood.
People come from all over the world because they know this is where the future is held.
The staff are very knowledgeable here, but don't worry, they won't make you disappear.

Occasionally they invite a star, like Tony Stockwell, from afar.
His knowledge is second to none, and he will help to show you how it's all done.

Stansted is a lovely hall, dedicated to people who know it all.
This is why they come here: to make their doubts disappear.
Stansted Hall is a lovely place, but when you leave, you leave no trace.
You take friendships that will last for years and knowledge that will bring people to tears.

Training here is second to none. The aim is to help you get your work done.
People tell me they don't believe in all that, but are amazed when I give them facts.
I see things that others can't, but I know I'm gifted where others aren't.
People come to me because they want to know what I can see.

I bring through relatives that have passed and give them evidence of
survival at last.

I tell them things that I couldn't possibly know, and they are amazed at
the show.
I bring through Mum and Dad, and Auntie Ruth. I tell them things,
which gives them proof.
When I give them solid proof, they know that I'm telling them the truth.

You have to be a bit different to go to Stansted Hall,
which was donated by Arthur Findlay to help us all.
I'm really glad he did this deed, and now don't find myself in need,
as most of the questions that I had have been answered thoroughly
indeed.

28

SPIRIT SIGHTINGS

I have had many spirit sightings in my life, my first real spirit sighting, happened in a farmhouse in Wales owned by an Irish lady. At the time I was working as a locksmith. She called me out and asked me if I could change all the locks on the house, as there'd been a problem with her and her husband—not my business to ask questions, just to comply with the customer's request. The actual farmhouse was located in a place called 100 House, an area outside Builth Wells. I was driving a transit van and had to travel down dirt tracks to locate this farmhouse.

It was a bumpy ride on a sunny day, and I was thinking how lucky I was to work on my own without anyone telling me what to do. I was guided to this lady's house knowing full well what she wanted me to do and that it would reap a decent financial reward.

I knew this because changing all the locks on the farm building was not going be cheap. It's not only the parts that cost money; it's also the intensive labour. And I knew that there would be many hours of work involved.

On arrival I was greeted by a very bubbly Irish lady, clearly from the south of Ireland. The building had been renovated to a good standard, and I could see that it had been done recently.

The windows were wooden and stained brown, quite modern, which would have been an expensive addition to the property. The lady owner had a most charming character and was fun to be withShe explained to me that she and her husband were no longer together. However, she knew where he had gone, and this was very much to her dissatisfaction.

I was invited in and asked if I would like tea. I was used to this hospitality, as I'd spent many years in Ireland with the military and found the people to be very hospitable, sociable, and extremely amusing with their stories and good cheer. The tea arrived. So did cake and biscuits. All of a sudden I was looking at a small banquet in front of me. She then insisted on getting out the family album and showing me what the house looked like before renovation.

As she got the album out and showed me the stages of renovation, it was evident that these were happier times in her life. I could see from the various stages of the renovation in the photographs that this had been a mean task; it must have taken months, if not years, to complete the work. It was all of a high standard, and she had to be congratulated on her achievement, which I did at the time, to her approval.

On completion of the tea-drinking, cake-eating, biscuit-dunking banquet that we were consuming amid my laughs at the things she was saying and stories she was telling, she suddenly said, 'Well, I suppose you better have a look around and see what needs doing, and let's get it done.'

So I went all around the house, looking at all the doors and windows, assessing her requirements. All this was written down, and I returned to the kitchen to report my findings.

I explained what needed doing and the cost of the work, but because of her hospitality I was prepared to make adjustments from my findings. This I did, and she was quite happy for me to carry on and do the work. I started straightaway and took the locks out and replaced them with new ones. I labelled up all of the keys and worked my way around the house.

My final door was a double French door leading from outside into the dining room, and to do this work I had to stand outside. I remember looking around and thinking what a lovely day it was, the sun shining and lambs playing in the fields. I had just started on the door when the lady came round and told me she was going to London now for the weekend. I explained I hadn't finished, but she told me to write out my bill and she would pay now, and asked me to put the keys through the front-door letter box when I finished. She was a very trusting person, but we felt we knew each other, and I must have had an honest face.

Invoice done, cheque received, I stood and watched her drive over the hill and down the track in the little white Suzuki jeep, thinking to myself that it didn't get much better than this, and wasn't it nice to do a job that you enjoyed, as I'm sure there aren't many that are in such a fortunate position. While I was working on the door of the empty room with not a care in the world, I saw that the room had no windows and no furniture— just a carpet on the floor and another door leading elsewhere.

And then, without any warning, I noticed as I bent down to my toolbox for a screwdriver that to my right was an elderly lady in a rocking chair.

I looked at her. The chair was on the ground, not hovering about or anything like that. She was solid. I couldn't see through her. Yet it was apparent to me that this was a ghost.

My first sighting. I just stood there looking at her. She didn't move. She just sat there looking at me. She was probably in her eighties. She was wearing a black Victorian-type dress with white lace around the collar, white lace around the cuffs, and black shoes with square buckles, and her hair was tied back with a black ribbon or band. Her appearance was very grey. I could see her eyes and the grey complexion of her face. She just sat looking at me, not moving.

What was there to be afraid of? This was a little old lady in a rocking chair, and as I now know, clearly a spirit person. Why was she there? Why did she appear to me? Well, the answer is that I was psychic and not aware of it. I hadn't known that I had the ability to see such things.

However, I did now. I couldn't believe it. I was quite pleased that there in front of me was a real spirit person. Everything I'd heard about them—how they are supposed to float around the room and such—wasn't happening. She just sat there. This was a truly magical moment in my life. I was witnessing a person from the past. *Fantastic*, I thought. Wouldn't it have been good if she had spoken to me? That would have been the icing on the cake, but she didn't. She just sat there looking. This made me wonder how many other spirit people had been around me that I had not noticed. I was lucky this time. I just happened to look up at the right time, and there she was.

It was a moment I will never forget. I can see her now as I write this. She just sat there looking at me, causing no harm to anyone. I could live with that. It would not have bothered me if she sat in my house. It would have been nice to see her if she appeared to me again, and yes, I would have tried to communicate with her. That might sound stupid, but if someone sits in front of you, as solid as she was, why not try?

I didn't move towards her, as I was sure she would have disappeared, and obviously she was no threat. I was just amazed. My next action, which baffles me to this day, was to pick up the screwdriver from the toolbox that I'd bent down to get in the first place. I picked it up and looked over to the old lady, but she had gone. I was alert for the rest of the time in the house, hoping to see her again, but unfortunately this was not to happen.

I completed the task at hand and locked the door from the outside, as I wouldn't consider entering someone's house when she wasn't there, and went round to the front door and placed the keys in the letter box as re-quested. I stood back and looked at the house and all the windows, hop-ing to get a glimpse of the old lady, but I couldn't see anything. I climbed into my van and drove off up the track back to the main road. The sun was still shining and the sheep were still playing in the fields. I'd been paid and I'd seen my first spirit person. What a wonderful day.

There have been many other signs of spirit people in my life, and it is clear to me that they appear when my mind is not focused on the thought of them being there. It's usually when I'm engrossed in something that they appear. Usually I catch sight of them in the corner of my eye, as I'm sure many of you do as well. You see movement. You may think to your-self, *What was that?* Yes, it was a spirit person. They move across door-ways, across rooms, sometimes slowly or sometimes quickly. I've even seen spirit animals, cats running across the room or across the doorway.

I know people who have even braked hard whilst driving a car because a spir-it stepped in front of them, and I know others who have experienced going straight through the person, having the shock and horror of the thought, *I've just run someone over.* They get out of their car and look back up the road, but there's no one there. They think they've just hit somebody that walked out in front of them, but no; no one is there. It was a spirit person.

Another occasion when I came into contact with a spirit person was when I was in France, where friends had moved house. They had bought a rather large bungalow with the best part of an acre of ground, including a large swimming pool in the back garden, one of those that is free-standing and must take a week to fill up with water—not the sort of thing you would like to be punctured in your back garden, as it would probably flood your house.

We drove down to Bordeaux, then left the motorway and went through the country roads and lanes until we found the village where they lived. We phoned them with the final directions and found the house. We were told that they were having a barbecue that afternoon. This suited me, a light barbecue, as it was midsummer and very hot, and we had driven a long way. Out came the cold beer and the red wine. What a mixture. Anyway, I hadn't drunk any and was asked to go down to the cellar and get the beer from the freezer. After being given directions, off I went.

There was a door that went into the cellar, just like you see in the movies, with a set of steps going down. There was a light switch that you had to switch on to see where you were going. It wasn't as bad as the films. It was painted white inside with a clean tiled floor and whitewashed walls. I got to the bottom of the stairs, and against the far wall was an upright freezer with a chest freezer, holding the beer, to its left. I walked across to the freezer and just happened to glance to my left, and there in the corner of the room stood a man.

He was about five feet tall, wearing a white tuxedo with a collar turned over at the top and a white silk Dickie bow tie. He had blond hair combed back, clearly greased. The difference between this person and the lady in a rocking chair was I could see through him. I could see the wall behind him. He was transparent: my first see-through spirit person.

Anyway, I looked at him. He looked like he was going to a ball or something, the way he was dressed, and he had this look on his face like someone you see in one of those Carrie Grant movies who usually turns out to be the villain. After studying this person I went to the freezer and opened it up, got the crate of beer out, shut the freezer door, and walked back across the room. The man was still there looking at me, so I walked up the stairs a few steps and then came back down again. He was still there looking at me.

I went back up the stairs, shut the door, and went back onto the veranda where the others were sitting with the barbecue now lit. 'You took your time,' I was told. I couldn't say a word because I knew that 1) I would probably be laughed at, and 2) if believed, my friend's wife would probably be on the next plane home, saying that she's not going to live there anymore.

That evening I was talking to my partner, and she said to me, 'You took your time getting that beer.' I said, 'Yes, I know,' and I told her what had happened. Her first reaction was, 'Whatever you do, don't tell Janet.' This was the wife of my friend who lived in the house.

We returned to England without a word being spoken about my encounter in their cellar. Approximately two months later, my brother phoned me on his mobile phone all the way from France. I had told him about my encounter, and he said, 'I'm in Ypres. They've got an old mock-up village here, a tourist attraction. You walk down this old street with doorways on either side. Behind one of the doorways is a bar where there are people sitting around tables. One of the tables has got a man in a white tuxedo the same height as you described. He's German.'

This could explain a lot, as the Germans had occupied this area during the Second World War. It is called Verdi-Sur-lot. This just goes to show that one doesn't imagine things; you see things for what they are, and if you have this experience yourself, please don't write it off as imagination, as this may well be an encounter with the spirit world. You should be pleased that they've come to visit you and tried to get your attention. It is nice just to know that they are there sometimes.

When I have talked about these experiences with other mediums, as I've said before, I've been told I'm lucky because not all mediums see spirits. I don't know why I do. However, I'm pleased I do, and there are certainly some people that I know have passed who I would love to meet again while I am still on the earth plane.

We all have questions that are unanswered. Can you imagine being able to communicate face-to-face with a spirit person and getting answers to questions that we all want to know? *What's it like in the spirit world? What do you do? Who have you met that I know?* Many questions.

When I reached the age of forty, I don't know why, but spirits and thoughts of passing occupied my mind quite a bit. I suppose that I had started to lose friends around me, people that I had thought would last forever, and then all of a sudden they were gone. And then I thought of my own passing: *What will happen to me? Will I be buried or cremated?* When I am looking round old graveyards purely for this reason, I notice the age of the occupants on the stones—'passed 1838'—and wonder who they were and what they did. You can tell by how grand the grave itself is if they were from a wealthy background or not, or if they were appreciated on the earth plane. You often see monuments like angels looking down or large granite boxes covering the grave, and sometimes writing all around about the person and his or her life.

It's always good to see this, because that person has not been forgotten. I know that in cremations you can now have a stone laid in the church-yard with the person's name on it and maybe the ashes underneath. I just feel personally that this is a cold way to go—obviously not really, when you think of the process. However, it just seems more loving with a burial, like people care; you are not forgotten. You're in one piece and at peace.

You often see people standing in graveyards talking to graves, giving the person the latest news from the family and loved ones about what's hap-pened, what's going on, who's done what. The deceased is still there. It gives comfort.

Another sighting of a spirit person was at an old Victorian house in Hereford. I was there to pick up my partner's daughter, Sarah, and her baby, Eva, and knocked on the door and was invited in. 'I won't be long,' I was told, so I stood in the hall looking at some pictures of London at night. One was a landscape picture. The lights were on, and I could see the Thames shining with all the streetlights reflecting along it. I just stood there looking, not thinking of anything in particular, and then I turned and looked around me. Once again, nothing special was on my mind. My eyes wandered up the stairs, and there, standing on the corner step, was a little girl probably eight years old, with long, blond, curly hair with ribbons, wearing a flowered dress, white socks, and shoes—clearly Victorian. I couldn't believe it. This was another spirit person. She just stood there looking at me. I looked at her. She looked at me. No movement from her, as with the lady in the rocking chair—just staring at me.

At this point Sarah came around the corner with a pram from the living room. I said, 'Sarah, come here quick. There is a little girl on the stairs there. Look.'

Sarah looked up and said, 'I can't see her.'

I pointed out that she was there on the bend of the stairs. 'Look.'

Sarah still said that she couldn't see her. I didn't believe it. How could I see her and Sarah could not? Anyway, we went towards the front door and I opened it and helped out with the pram. When Sarah got to the bottom of the steps, I looked up, and there, still on the corner of the stairs, was the little girl looking at me. I couldn't believe it, what I'd seen and Sarah hadn't. This was amazing. *I must have some power or gift that others don't have,* I thought. This was confirmation. It was the first time I'd been with someone else when a sighting had come up.

I learned something from this experience: I tend to see spirits when my mind is in a neutral state, if that's the word—not thinking about anything specifically. This is when it happens. This is when I see them.

I had a request from a friend who owns an old vicarage. He said that he had been doing some work on his house and thought he had disturbed a ghost. He was well-aware that he had a spirit presence in house, as it had been commented on by other members of the family. He asked me if I would have a look. Well, of course I would, although not knowing what to expect.

I arrived at the house and went in after talking for about half an hour and drinking several cups of tea. I was asked if I would walk around and see if I sensed anything. I said of course, though I had never done this before. But there's a first time for everything. We walked down the hall and got to the bottom of the stairs. As I looked up, I could see a man standing there looking at me, a spirit person in a white shirt, sleeves rolled up, looking at me. I said, 'Brian, there is a man at the top of the stairs. I think he's the one you're looking for.' And I described him. He said that's what people had seen before.

Then I walked up the stairs. He disappeared as I got to the top. Then Brian pointed to a bedroom that this person had been seen in. I said, 'Okay. I will have a look.' I walked to the door and opened it and walked into cobwebs, a thick mass of cobwebs across the doorway. I was trying to walk through it; if you've ever done that, you know what I mean. I'd heard of this before, but this was the first time I'd encountered it myself. I was trying to wipe the cobwebs off my face and my hair, but there was nothing there that you could see. It was certainly there, but not visible.

And then there he was in the corner of the room. Brian was apprehensive about coming in, so I told him to stay where he was and shut the door. This could have been a mistake, because the spirit person came towards me. 'Get out, get out,' I was told.

I then realised all of a sudden that I was not just clairvoyant but clairaudient. I could hear spirit as well as see them. He came up to me. I stood my ground, and he pushed me. I rocked backwards and then returned to the upright position. He pushed me again, saying, 'Get out, get out.' Clearly he knew I could see and hear him. Brian stood at the door, and I said to him, 'Look at this. He's trying to push me out of the room.'

Brian witnessed me being pushed by the spirit person. I was rocking backwards and forwards. I stood with my legs in a stance, like a boxer starts, one forward and one off to the rear. I wasn't going to fall over. It was clear this spirit person could be aggressive. However, I didn't feel that he meant to harm anyone; he just didn't want our presence..

I retreated from the room, closed the door, and said to Brian, 'Did you see that?' He said yes. Brian still lives in the house today. I don't feel the spirit bothers him, as he can't see the man like I could, and I know that the man knew he couldn't see him either, so didn't bother him. A strange situation, but these things happen.

I was staying at my brother's house in Cambridge, England, with my partner, as we were invited to stay with him instead of in the usual hotel accommodation. I'm not a fan of staying in other people's houses, as I prefer hotels, which give more freedom to come and go, move around, and use the facilities as you wish.

Anyway, we were sleeping in a double bed in the back room of my brother's house when things started happening. I became aware of a little boy and then a little girl, who pestered me all night. I didn't get much sleep, as they were very disturbing. They were crying and making a fuss. I couldn't believe what was going on. It wasn't a dream. It was actually happening. Anyway, I put up with it for the night. Then, the following morning when I got up, my brother and his wife, Pat, were downstairs in the kitchen. I walked in and said, 'That's the last time I'm staying up there. I was kept awake all night by a little boy and a little girl.'

And my brother said, 'Pat had two miscarriage. One was a boy and one was a girl.'

I said, 'I can tell you they're still there.' That was the last time I slept in that house. If I go and visit him now, I always book into paid accommodation.

Recently I was sitting having dinner with my partner, and I got up from the dining table and walked towards the kitchen to take the plates out. As I turned from the dining room to the kitchen door, which is at a sideways angle to the dining room, there stood round the corner by the door a spirit person, a full-body apparition. I could see everything. He had brown hair sticking up on the top, slightly spiky—you know, sticking up while lying down, like when you've got up in the morning and you're having a bad hair day. This person was about five feet six inches tall, and his clothes were brown in colour. I saw him for maybe one or two seconds. He was only a couple of feet away from me, and suddenly he disappeared.

I looked round the doorway at my partner, who was still sitting at the dining table, and said there'd been a spirit person standing there. I'd nearly walked into him. She asked what he looked like. I described him as above and asked her if she had seen this one before. She said that she hadn't. I had to ask this question, as we have at least three spirit people in our house, which doesn't worry me. Why should it? They walked on the earth plane and didn't worry anyone then. So why should they now?

I'm sure many of you have the same type of experiences that I do. You see spirits one minute, and then they're gone. People say these are just flashbacks from the past. Well, I don't believe it. I think they are with us because they clearly liked the place when they were here on the earth plane, and now they haven't gone back to the spirit world. They see no reason why they should change things.

Many people say that they are grounded and need help to pass over to the spirit world. Well, how do people know this? I have brought through people in readings, people that have passed the day before.

29

MARTIN

I talked earlier about when I first met Tony Stockwell and how he brought my friend Martin through during a reading—the one who passed by his own hand, Tony said. Martin was a very good friend of mine. He had problems. He was a manic depressive. In his younger years he'd been fit and healthy with a good physique, quite the outdoor type. Canoeing, climbing, hill walking, weight lifting—he did lots of physical things like this until one day his sister was having a problem with a local biker that she was dating. Things weren't well between the two of them. Martin went to the pub to talk to him. The biker tried to make out that nothing was wrong and bought Martin a drink. Unfortunately for Martin, he had put something in it that would change his life.

Martin became very ill. Whatever had been put in the drink affected this bright young man, turning him into a different person from the one that had walked into that pub. His confidence was gone, as well as his abilities. He then became depressed, put on weight—lots of it—and was a shadow of his former self. What had this person done to him? I know who the

person is. However, I will not name him in this book. The person supposedly passed to the spirit world a while ago, but there have been sightings
of him, which tells me he hasn't—as the saying goes, like a bad penny.

Martin lived in a house owned by his parents, and he was a keen Land
Rover enthusiast and biker. He was unable to work due to his depression
and lived on benefits. This went against the grain with Martin. He hated
it. He wanted to work like everyone else, but they wouldn't let him. He
was unable to take the responsibility. However, he was still allowed to
drive a car and ride a motorbike. I had a Harley-Davidson at the time and
so did Martin. We would go to bike shows and ride outs. It was always
fun being with him because you never knew what was going to happen
next.

Martin also liked camping, which was something we did together. I remember our first trip. He said we'd sleep out under the stars. This was
nothing to me, as I'd spent most of my time in the army camping.

On this particular trip, all I took with me was a shelter sheet. This
is like a green waterproof tarpaulin that you hang from the tree by
the top, like a tent, and lie underneath to stay dry—no sides and no
ends. Martin built one next to me, and there we were, at one with nature. Martin had brought his camper van with him, which was an old
Volkswagen with a high top. He loved that van. He went everywhere
in it. He cooked a meal in the camper van and shouted to me, 'Grub's
ready!' I was expecting beans on toast, but he'd prepared this gourmet
meal with red wine and everything. I was amazed. I hadn't realised
he could cook like he did.

Anyway, night-time came and we got in our sleeping bags. We were lying there looking up at the stars at the end of the shelter sheet when I

heard the camper van door open. It was a side sliding door, and then it slammed shut. I looked up and the light came on. There was Martin making his bed up in the camper. So much for 'back to nature.' I stayed where I was. This was my second home. I was enjoying it. Clearly Martin wasn't going to give up his home comforts, his cosy campervan and his warm bed.

We went out one day on a bike ride to Brecon in Wales. There was a museum there exhibiting the battle of Rorke's Drift, when just over 150 British and colonial soldiers had stood firm against thousands of South African Zulus. They'd stood their ground day and night and been attacked by a massive, overwhelming number of Zulus. Figures were estimated at four thousand. However, they'd held their position and not been taken. As the sun rose on the final day, the hills all around the mission station were covered in Zulus. There were only two officers in charge, who were convinced that this was the end. However, the Zulus instead honoured them with songs, as they had been brave warriors that fought a brave fight. The Zulus knew they could take the compound and slaughter everyone inside; however, they didn't. They left them and retreated away.

Eleven Victoria Crosses, the highest award to be received in the British Empire, were awarded that day, and this museum had many pieces from the battle. Martin and I walked round and looked at everything. We talked to the curator, who was amazed at Martin's knowledge, as he was a very knowledgeable person and sometimes quite pleasing to be with when intellectual opinions on a subject were required.

I noticed that opposite this museum there was a café, and I said to Martin that I would buy him lunch. Always ready for a free meal, he agreed. We went in and were presented with the menus. I ordered a plain omelette, and Martin ordered something on the menu called a gut buster. When the waitress came to take our order and he asked for the gut buster, she said, 'That's disgusting.' I didn't know whether she meant the meal or Martin! When it arrived, it was just one big heap of everything covered in chips— a massive plate of cholesterol.

Martin consumed this meal in no time at all and then asked me if I was going to eat my chips. I said I wasn't, and he ate them as well. Then he asked to see the dessert menu, which I said I'd give a miss but told him to carry on with, and he did. I paid the bill and we left the café. As we were walking up the street, Martin erupted in violent flatulence. I thought this was just a typical day out with Martin. Those days are sadly missed.

I remember another time we were out on our Harleys. We had been to Hay-on-Wye and were returning to Hereford. We were riding along a country road. Martin was in front of me and there was a car in front of him, but there was also a car coming the other way. Just as the two cars closed towards each other, Martin overtook the car in front. How he got in the gap between the two cars I'll never know. I wasn't aware at the time that this was an attempt to end it all. Can you imagine what it would have done to those poor people driving those cars, and of course me, as an observer of the whole event?

The problem with suicide is the people it leaves behind. On that note, if only I'd known, maybe I could have done something, perhaps talked to him—anything to keep him alive. But unfortunately he was determined to go to the spirit world early. It was his wish, but I know his mind wasn't good. If he hadn't had that drink and whatever was in it, he would still be alive today. In Spiritualism there are seven basic principles. Number six is compensation and retribution hereafter for all the good and evil deeds done on earth.

Retribution Indeed

Martin had been going to a local gun club. He couldn't have a firearms licence because of his condition, but he could have an air pistol, one that worked with a little CO_2 cartridge and wouldn't hurt anyone, just for shooting at paper targets from about ten feet away. Anyway, what I didn't know was that someone in the club had let him fire a .22 rifle. It wasn't known by many that Martin had a problem; otherwise he would have never been allowed. Somehow he managed to sneak some of the ammunition into his pocket. Also without anybody's knowledge, he acquired a .22 smooth-barrelled shotgun. This is the sort of thing farmers use for killing rats on their farms—a very weak shotgun. However, Martin found out that it would also fire live ammunition.

Martin had a lodger staying at his house. The lodger had a job and used to go to work first thing in the morning. He went to work one morning and returned home at the usual time of six o'clock. He noticed that the lights in and outside the house were not on. This was unusual because they were always on. He also had a motorbike, and he parked it on the drive. He went through the back door as always, and there in the utility room was Martin's dog scratching at the door to get into the living room. He thought something must be wrong and wondered why the dog was in there. It must have been there all day. He opened the door and the dog ran into the main house and up the stairs to Martin's bedroom. He followed the dog up the stairs and opened the bedroom door.

There, lying on the bed, was Martin. He had taken the .22 shotgun, loaded a live round, lain on the bed, and shot himself in the head at point-blank range. No one knows if he passed to Spirit instantly. This has always been a concern of mine. We will never know. Obviously, because firearms were involved in the death, the police were called in and an investigation started. I was asked to give a statement, as I knew Martin very well. The lodger was devastated, and I know it still affects him to this day, as they were good friends.

An inquest was held and it was a suicide verdict. He had taken his own life because of depression. How sad. I was asked by his mother if I would say a few words at the funeral because she didn't want someone who would break down and cry and ruin Martin's day by being weak. I agreed. However, I was told that she wanted to hear what I was going to say and vet it before I delivered the eulogy. My eulogy was edited several times by her, and at the last minute my time to deliver the speech was reduced, so no pressure there.

The funeral was massive. Martin had a lot of friends. It was requested that we ride our motorbikes behind the hearse and that Martin's helmet be placed on top of his coffin. His mother agreed to this, provided that the funeral home was okay with it. They agreed. We arrived at the church with a large entourage of motorcycles following behind the coffin. We stopped all the traffic in the town on the roundabouts so Martin could pass uninterrupted. He would have loved this attention, with everyone running around for him. He would have loved to have been that important. There was standing room only in the church, and there were speakers outside transmitting what was said into the microphone inside. The whole churchyard, full of people who had turned up to the funeral, heard what was being said.

The time came when I had to give my eulogy. This was a celebration of Martin's life, and I was going to tell it how it was. I wasn't going to say wonderful things about this mild, kind, quiet person who wasn't. I would tell it exactly as it was—the real Martin. Everybody there knew him. If I'd said anything else, the place would have fallen apart with laughter. That wasn't Martin. So I told it like it was. I talked about the trip to the café, and I talked about other things that we had done, and everybody laughed and clapped, as that's how they remembered him. He would have been proud.

It was a huge funeral. We all then retired to a local pub where they played DVDs of him on the big screen. Some days later I was asked by his mother to come around to the house, as they were sorting out Martin's things, and she asked me if there was anything I would like of Martin's. I said that I had everything I needed; I had the memories. She seemed surprised that I didn't want to go through his things and take mementos of his life. I did look through his photo albums and was amazed at pictures of him up mountains, in deep snow, out climbing—things I'd never known he'd done—and the pictures of him in the weight lifter's leotard, pressing weights on a bench. He was clearly a fit, strong lad when he was younger. How sad, what he'd become—sad for himself that he was no more what he was before.

Anyway, we were sitting around his dining room table. I sat with my back to the window, his mother opposite me and his father with his back to the patio doors to my right. We were discussing Martin, and I don't know why, but I kept looking over to my left, as there was a doorway that led into the hall and you could see about five steps of the stairs that went up to the bedrooms. I had been sitting there for about an hour talking about various things, and I kept looking at this doorway. I kept getting drawn in that direction.

And then, suddenly, I looked at the stairs and there came down a black shape. It looked like a person, but there were no features. The shape was there, but it was jet black, like someone had got a hold of a rubber balloon and pulled it out of shape, distorted. I remember thinking, *Oh no, don't let it come in here.* What would I do? I could see it and they couldn't. They would think I'd gone mad. Suppose it came up to me and touched me! What would I do? This was probably the worst situation I'd ever been in in my life.

I watched in sheer horror. It had to be Martin. *Don't do this to me, mate. I thought I was your friend. I don't need this.* Can you imagine his parents' reaction? I can. Anyway, it didn't come in. It went into the front room and must have gone through the door, because I didn't hear it open. In the front room was Martin's computer and all his books and photos. It was like an office. I can see why it went in there.

I just sat there looking at the door, thinking, *No. I've got to get out of here. This is going to be too much.* So I made my excuses, shook hands, and left straightaway. I was glad to be out. I didn't want to go through that.

Why he appeared like he did I don't know. It was not like all the other spirit people that I had seen, normal-looking as they had been whilst on the earth plane. No, it was this black shape. Why? I was baffled. Every day I have to drive past Martin's house to go to work, and I look up at the window on the front that used to be his bedroom window, where it happened, and I say, 'Morning, Martin. How are you?' Always thinking of why he's not here. What could I have done to prevent this? Could I have stopped this happening?

Why didn't he talk to me? I was his friend. He could have told me. I could have talked to him and maybe got him to see sense. I understand from his lodger that he didn't want to see forty. He was thirty-nine when he killed himself. What was it about forty? Maybe he felt that this age marked the end of his life, and that he couldn't do anything after this age. Well, Martin, I feel you were wrong. You're sadly missed by good friends. And if you, the reader have been in this situation yourself, I'm sure that you felt exactly the same. *What could I have done to prevent this?* The unanswered question.

One morning as I was driving past Martin's house, which was still empty—it hadn't been sold—I looked up to say, 'Morning, Martin.' The Louvre blinds that were in his bedroom were at a slight angle and I could see into the room, and there behind the blinds was a person. It was Martin, looking out at me—that black shape. He was still there and always will be. His mother put the house up for sale and it was bought by a family. I don't know if they know the story, but I guarantee Martin won't leave them alone. He'll let them know he's there, because one thing he liked was a good practical joke, and I dare say he will play a few on them.

I was given a message when I was at a Spiritual church. The medium who brought Martin through said that he said, 'Forget about me and get on with your lives.' This was typical of Martin. But how could you forget such a person?

I was at the cemetery in Hereford at Whitecross. This is a massive cemetery. People have been put there since the eighteenth century. My partner and I were visiting a grave. I was walking towards one of the rubbish bins with some dead flowers that I had taken off the grave to replace with new ones. As I walked down a path towards this, I was shouted at by a lady in a dressing gown. I looked and realised straightaway this was a spirit person. She said, 'My bunions are all right now. They don't hurt anymore. I'm okay.' She said, 'They don't come to visit me, my son and my daughter. They're all grown up now, got children of their own, and they don't come here.

'My husband is with me now. It's Father's Day today.' That was the reason I was there. She said, 'There are no flowers on our grave.' I looked at her as she stood there. Then my partner shouted at me, 'What are you look-ing at?'

'This lady here in a dressing gown tells me her bunions are okay now.'
'I can't see her,' said my partner.

'No, I know you can't. You're not psychic,' I said quietly. I know the lady knew I could see her, though.

Another sighting I had was when I visited the American War Cemetery in Cambridge, England. During World War II there was a massive American presence in Cambridgeshire, Norfolk, Suffolk, and the counties of Lincolnshire. All around these areas were many airfields. From bomb-er commands to fighter squadrons, they were there, and as we all know, many bombing raids were carried out on Germany from these areas.

Unfortunately, many lives were lost. These young men who flew these large aircraft, with not many flying hours to their credit, went on raids in Germany and Europe and never came back, or if they did, they passed in what was left of the aircraft they were flying in.

I suppose because of the logistics of returning their remains to America, many of them had to be buried on UK soil. This was certainly the case in Cambridge, and as a result a very large American cemetery is full of these young men who passed during this conflict. As I said before, there's some-thing about cemeteries that has always interested me. Who were these people? How old were they when they passed? And how did they pass?

They should never be forgotten. Their efforts could never be rewarded to the value of giving their own lives. These were true heroes who flew day and night knowing full well that they may never return. There are lots of stories of them living life to the fullest when they were in England. I don't blame them. They knew what was coming. How can people praise war when such horrible, tragic things happened to all those young men, and in many cases women as well?

I was visiting my brother in Cambridge and said that I would like to go to the American Cemetery, as I'd never been there before and I wanted to see how they had been remembered. It's an impressive place and worth a visit if you are ever in the area. I can't help but feel moved by these places. On arrival at the cemetery we parked outside and walked in. It is a huge place with many white crosses showing the names and when they passed.

As I had thought, there were very young men in their late teens and early twenties whose lives had hardly started, but now there they were. I walked among the stones, looking at the names and where they came from, what they were—mostly air crew. It didn't take much imagination to think of how horrific their injuries must have been. There are no other words: they'd buried what was left of these human beings.

There is a church, or something more like a hall, in this cemetery, where there are flags and books explaining who the occupants are and what went on. A very grand building. This was built by the Americans, as the UK never seems to spend this much money on anything that doesn't make money. Maybe we can take a lesson from this. We should give great respect to our war dead, as they are the only reason that we are here today and not under occupation by a dictator. Anyway, I had a good look round at the flags, the building, and the structure, and marvelled at how it had all been put together, then slowly walked out into the daylight.

I walked down the steps and looked across to my right at the gravestones, and there I saw an airman in a brown flying suit, wearing big flying boots and brown leather headgear with wires coming out of it and a face-mask attached. He was standing by a gravestone and staring across the graveyard.

He just stared forward, but his gaze was fixed on something in the distance. I just stood there looking at him. No one else noticed him. No one else could see him. My brother, his wife, Pat, and my partner were all there. They couldn't see him. Only I could. I stared at him for a while and studied him without moving. He was solid. I couldn't see through him, unlike the man in the cellar in France. Still no movement. I stood looking and not moving myself. I didn't want to frighten him away, as I was enjoying his presence. I felt like I was back in the day when it was all happening, because he was as real as life, though really a spirit person.

I started walking towards him down the rest of the steps and onto the grass. He must have sensed I was there, for he disappeared right in front of my eyes, gone. I walked up to the gravestone that he'd been standing next to and looked at the writing on the grave. It said that it was the grave of a young airman and gave the year of passing, during the Second World War.

We walked among the graves once again, looking at the names, the ages. These were someone's sons who never returned. One thing always strikes me when I visit these places, which I have done many times. I've been round the First World War graves in France and Belgium and the Second World War graves in Omaha Beach and the large cemetery above, and I always feel moved. I recently visited the graveyard in Hereford, England, where there is a special area set aside for members of the 22 Special Air Service (SAS) Regiment.

Many of the people that have been laid to rest there I knew personally, and when I stand at the graves I can't help but think of the times we had, good and bad, and always the way they passed—some of them at violent hands, some by accident. It is the nature of their training that there will be accidents, and there are. Even on the selection course people passed to the spirit world. One did on mine, and recently three more of them passed on a selection course for this famous regiment.

I see their faces as I remembered them at the age they were when they passed. There is a wall with stone plaques that runs on the right-hand side of this special area. These plaques have the names of members of the regiment who couldn't be returned during the Falklands campaign. Eighteen members of the regiment died all at once in a helicopter crash, which was a devastating time for all. Their names are recorded on this wall because their bodies could never be recovered from the bottom of the South Atlantic Ocean. I knew all of these people and knew them well, and as I said before, one of them was Geordie, the reason I joined the SAS. They were brave men who went a little bit further and shall never be forgotten.

I noticed on my last visit to this cemetery that outside the regimental plot, as it is known, was one ex-member. His name was Frank Collins. Frank served in B Squadron. He was in the air troop and I was in the mobility unit. Frank was not a religious person at first, until he went on an exchange to Delta Force in the states. On his return he had found religion, from where I don't know. He wouldn't have a word said against religion of any sort. I even remember him one day telling someone not to take the Lord's name in vain—totally out of character for him. It made me think, *What's happened to him? Where is all this coming from?*

And then he left the army and wasn't interested in military life anymore. I couldn't believe it. There he was, jumping out of planes having a good time, and all of a sudden he throws it all in. What was going on? And then one day I saw him walking up the road in a dog collar. 'Frank,' I said, 'what's all this about?'

He said, 'I've got the church of St James now.' This was a local area of Hereford.

'So what's going on?'

He replied, 'You'll see.'

I had to find out what Frank was doing. Suddenly he was a vicar. And then I heard through the grapevine—'jungle drums,' as it's known in Hereford—that Frank wanted to be the regimental padre. This meant he would be commissioned to the rank of captain and have freedom to move where he wanted to visit all parts of the world where the regiment served, going with them in many cases and jumping out of as many planes as he wanted to, getting involved in lots of training.

Not long after learning this, I spoke to a senior member of the regiment who I'd served with and told him what I'd heard. His answer was, 'That will never happen.'

I said, 'No?'

He said again, 'That will never happen.' It was clear to me that Frank had upset somebody along the line, and he was clearly treading on somebody's toes. Something was wrong. I felt this was a crying shame, as Frank was such a dedicated person. He would have made a good regimental padre; however, it was not to be.

I never saw Frank again, as he moved away and I never had a chance to talk to him. He must have heard from somebody what had been said, but it certainly wasn't me. As we say in Hereford, he went off radar for a while, and then one day the news came through that Frank had committed suicide, taken his own life. Why?

And for some reason, to add insult to injury, they hadn't buried him in the regimental plot but elsewhere—though not far from the plot, so you can't miss it when you're looking. We are very strange in the UK. We don't seem to look after our veterans, unlike in America, where they do. We have them living on the streets, suffering mental illness and drink problems, many incarcerated. No one helps them. I feel so sorry for them. They are all proud men and women who have served their country, and to be treated like that is a disgrace. There is a true saying: 'Charity begins at home.' And I wish that it did. These individuals should be helped to get back on track with the dignity and understanding that they need.

I hear people say that it was their career choice. However, people join the forces for many different reasons, and career doesn't always enter into it. Many times it's to leave violent homes or a violent area that they live in and would never be able to escape otherwise, or to become good individuals and good team members. They become educated, which they could have never done before, and in many cases they put themselves in harm's way without thinking about the consequences, and often pay the price.

Graves of the Brave

I look across the fields. I see the crosses white.
They shine like marble in the daytime light.
But light is what we all need, without a doubt.
Unfortunately for them, their lights have gone out.

The names are all there, bold and bare:
Corporal Smith, Captain Blair,
Sergeant Johnson, and Lance Corporal Ware.
The regiments are different, none of them the same.
However, it doesn't matter now,
as there isn't anyone left to blame.

These aren't graves of individuals, you know that for a fact,
as you've seen the old films on the telly that certainly dispute that.
The truth is that many individuals were put into one hole.
It's all that could be done, God bless their souls.

Officers and men, there is no difference in the end.
They all die the same.
We could spend years pointing the blame.
Need and greed make men bleed,
And politicians will have their way,
but who will pay?
Not them, for sure. They're not going to risk going to war.
Problems have happened in countries ever since time began.
Why do we have to put our nose in?
Just because we can?

Martin

We don't need World War Three.
That's the lesson indeed.
Haven't we learned about the need for greed?
Death and destruction is all that will come out of this,
or maybe an abyss.

These graves of the brave, they send us a warning
so that we can be saved.
Don't ignore the warning, whatever you say,
or these could be the graves of us one day.

30

SPIRITUAL CHURCHES

I am going to talk about Spiritual churches, as there are many of them around, all run by volunteers, some run better than others. Like in any other organisation, one needs to be an organiser to head one of these churches. I've been in many. They are run at different levels of confidence and ability, but I've always found that goodwill and enthusiasm will win the day.

Spiritual churches have congregations like other religions. They have guest mediums on a regular basis. These mediums can be of mixed ability; by this I mean that some are very good and give detailed information to the recipient. Others who have clearly been doing it for many years aren't that good, as they seem to have this set script that they play out. They start with an opening prayer, which will go on forever. There is no set prayer like in other churches; the medium writes his own prayer. Also, some of these people when giving a reading to a member of the audience rely on their psychic abilities rather than a spiritual connection, which

I've found through experience, as a member of the audience, doesn't always work.

When you are progressing in the world of mediumship, it's good to attend these churches, as it gives you an idea of what not to do and how not to present yourself. This is why I can recommend the Arthur Findlay College of Mediumship at Stansted, Essex. As I said before, there you learn the correct way to do everything: what you can say and what you can't say, and how to put things over to recipients, which you can't learn in these Spiritual churches. As we know, many people who go to Spiritual churches are looking for answers about a lot of situations in their lives, which can be a very sensitive situation. The last thing they need is someone handling the situation very badly, especially where a bereavement is involved, and even more so with the loss of a child.

As I've said, I've visited many of these churches and worked the platform in quite a few. I've always had people approaching me afterwards asking for private readings, wanting me to elaborate more on what I have said to them, and I have always been asked by the church to return and do it all again, as they were impressed with my performance. I know this sounds like I'm blowing my own trumpet; however, I was initially taught correctly.

I've seen many mediums giving general information in churches, stating to the recipient that there is a situation around him or her at the moment that needs sorting out; he or she is unsure of which way to turn. This statement would relate, I'm sure, to every one of us. We all have situations around us all the time that need sorting out. Be it at work or at home, there is always something going on that needs answers.

The other statement I've heard a lot is, 'You are at a crossroads in your life. You don't know which way to turn. You could do with some help.' This once again relates to us all. We are at a crossroads all the time, and always wondering what the future holds: Where are we going? What is coming next? Will we be lucky in work, in love? Will we win the lottery? It's endless, so what I'm saying is that I feel that there is a lot of generalising.

I was in the church once when a lady medium was giving a reading to a member of the audience, and she said to him, 'Don't you wish that you hadn't left college, and that you'd finished your education?' The person in question looked at her and said, 'But I'm only thirteen.'

This was a classic example of someone doing mediumship without the spirit link. It made that medium look quite inferior, and everything else she said from then on was unbelievable. I work with Spirit, and I find it's the only way that communicators will show you situations and information that cannot be contested. This is the only way to do it. I have found it is really satisfying when the reading goes well, for both parties. I'm sure the communicator who sees his or her message interpreted correctly for the correct person is glad.

I've seen situations where mediums hang around outside the church in the smoking area, listening to conversations and picking up on them and then bringing up parts of them to the audience. This is absolutely unforgivable. If they can't do it, they shouldn't be there. I would never do this. If there is no link, I will say there is no link.

I remember a time when I was reading for my local church and I had a girl of only about ten years come through. She stood there in a blue swimming costume with a frilly neck and frilly arms, and I said to the recipient that I had a girl here, and I described her and said, 'She tells me she's ten years old at this time.' This was a memory link of a happier time in this child's life. I told the recipient that this child had passed at an older age of around nineteen years, and that she had attended the casualty department prior to passing. I said that it was known that she would pass. The recipient said this was not the case, and that I only knew who this person was because I'd recently seen the recipient at the graveyard by her grave.

This was not the case. I had been there visiting a relative's grave, but quite a way off from where she was, and had not recognised her, as she had cut her hair quite a bit and I was concentrating on what I was doing, which was tending the grave of someone who had passed.

If she had let me continue, I could have told her what else I saw. However, I was not allowed to do this, and I ended the link, I'm sure much to the displeasure of the communicator and certainly myself. This person professes to be a medium herself. I find it very sad that she would not listen to the message that her daughter had clearly come to tell her, and that message was of how she passed.

As I said before, I have met some very good mediums in the past, and one that I have great respect for, who is in Kidderminster, is Michelle Emery. Michelle is a very gifted medium. I first saw her on platform at a Spiritualist church, and I was amazed at her abilities and went to speak to her afterwards. I couldn't help but feel this fantastic energy coming from her. Every time she came to church I would make sure I was there. I eventually managed to join her circle, which was a close circle at her home.

Every time I got up to speak in her house to give a reading to one of the circle members, the speed of the reading was really quick. It was as if I were being boosted along by some magic force, and if I sat near her I would feel an energy coming into me—truly remarkable. And she is a truly remarkable person. I haven't found this with any other medium that I have met. There is no doubt about it that this lady will go far and be extremely well-known in the world of mediumship.

I know that you are now wondering, I'm sure, *How do I tell a true medium?* But it's quite simple: don't give them any information whatsoever, and let them tell you what your situation is. All that is happening around you, they should be able to pick out, in many cases along with detailed information like names, relationships, height, hair colour, age, and occupation.

All this information should flow naturally from the medium. You know mediums know what they are talking about when they have a spiritual link. As I said before, it is quite easy to look at somebody and see if they are overweight or if they've got a walking stick or have other problems and point these things out. These are all visual. It doesn't mean they know. These things are obvious. That's not mediumship; that's observation. But to tell someone, for instance, 'I have your eleven-year-old son here. He tells me his name is Stephen, and he passed on a motorbike whilst fooling around with others on waste ground, and yes, he wasn't wearing a crash helmet,' tells you without doubt or question that this medium has a link, unless of course you are known to him or her, which is always a risk when you have people reading locally, especially in small towns or villages. And if a medium is that good, he or she will be able to tell you much more with regards to other things in your life that only you would know.

I remember once I was at the church and we were doing table readings. There were six of us invited for this evening of table readings. My first reading was for a young lady around nineteen years old. She sat in front of me, and I said, 'Who's James?' She jumped to her feet and said, 'Wow, I don't believe it. That's my boyfriend.' And then I saw behind her a tall building with a spire on top. This was a symbol Spirit showed to me for university. I said to her, 'You're going to university.' She just looked and said, 'Yes.' And then I saw a road by the sea with a roundabout and gates to the right, and I said, 'You are going to Cardiff University.'

Once again she jumped up to her feet with the same expression on her face. I couldn't believe I could do this. I said, 'James is going to university as well—however, not the same one. Yes, it's back the other way along the coast. In fact, it's Bristol.' She was amazed. How could I do this? She'd never seen it before. I had a true spirit link, and I was shown all the information and was able to pass it on to her. I was then able to tell other things about her life that made her very happy, and not only that, but with the information I had given her at the beginning, she knew it would all be true.

I remember giving a reading in church to another medium. This is unusual in churches because most mediums for some unknown reason don't like reading for other mediums. I suppose it is this fear that they may get it wrong. I've never had this problem. If I've got the spirit link, I know the words I say will be true. On this particular occasion I told the medium in front of all the congregation that I had a father with me, and that he'd shown me a maroon-coloured lorry, and I told her how many children were in the family, which I believe was seven. She confirmed that this was all true and that she remembered the lorry. I said, 'You will remember, then, that your dad did what he could to earn a living.'

To this she said, 'Yes, he did.' And he showed me himself wearing a white shirt, with the sleeves rolled up. This to me was a symbol of a working man, one that works with his hands. I was also told that life in her house was like the television programme *The Darling Buds of May*, like the family, called the Larkins. She smiled and said, 'Yes, that's exactly how it was.'

'I know,' I said. 'I can see it.' There was this video of her life as a child running in front of me. It was like I was watching it on a television set.

That's how I see things when I work with Spirit, and it is all in colour, not black and white. She approached me afterwards and said, 'You were spot-on. That's exactly how it was in our house, and I have fond memories of my childhood.' I looked at her as she smiled. I envied her. I wished mine had been like hers. There was a true love for her parents, and they truly loved their children, just like on television.

I've also seen mediums stand up and say, 'Right. Everyone's getting a reading today.' How can they say that? How do they know that everyone will get a link? It just doesn't happen. This tells me straightaway what we are going to get: generalisation. It is clear with these kinds of people that it is well-practised; it is like a script that they run through, and generally everyone gets the same target reading, the same words that slightly change. They are generalising all the time.

Every time I hear this I feel like saying, 'Right. I'm off, can't listen to this.' Sitting there for an hour listening to someone generalising is not my idea of mediumship, and oh, the amount of times I've heard mediums say to people, 'You see Spirit, don't you? You should be up here doing this. You've got what it takes.' The person might be frightened of standing up and talking to people. Not everyone is able to do it, just as not everyone is a leader; many are followers, good at listening to instruction and doing as instructed.

The problem with these people is that they generalise, but things they are telling people can be life changing in many situations. This is why when I started in mediumship I didn't want to be classed as one of those, so I researched it and asked the right people about how I could get qualified and how I could be certified as genuine, because many, many mediums aren't. I was advised to join the SNU, which is the Spiritualists National Union. It's not a trade union, but a union of Spiritualists who have been trained and tested. Their abilities have been proven on many occasions in front of their peers. This was the only way I would go forward, and through the Arthur Findlay College I achieved this.

It is like a university: it's all right saying you have got a degree, but when you show the paperwork that backs it up, you are looked upon differently by the person questioning your abilities. Unfortunately, life is like this. We all need paperwork to back up our abilities. Believe me, SNU standards are high.

Isn't it sad that in life we have to do this? But there are so many copies around: of designer clothes, shoes, and goods—even electrical goods. can catch fire if left on. You would think that people who have the ability to do this, like master criminals, would run legitimate businesses and make far more money out of it,. If they only ran a proper business, how well-off would they be. people who mastermind big robberies or con people out of thousands of pounds. S

Spiritual churches aren't always great buildings. Some are tin huts in villages, but they're all Spiritual churches bonded by enthusiastic people that keep a spiritual community together with great enthusiasm, always with little funding, if any at all, but still having to pay for the guest medium and sometimes the use of the village hall and the tea and biscuits always supplied—hence a small entrance fee to cover the expenses. These churches will never be rich, nor would they want to be. They put on events throughout the year: Harvest Festival, Remembrance Day, Christmas, Easter. They are always there gathering people together. If it's somebody's birthday and it's known about, it will be remembered.

This recognition of birthdays for people that live on their own and have no relatives at all gives a feeling of belonging. There is always a shoulder when they need it, and always a member or two to come round and

228

help them sort out the basic things in life that they are unable to do for themselves.

I remember being the medium in one of these churches in Wales. It was a little tin hut. You could smell the damp. There was a carpet on the floor that had seen better days. The furniture was old and basic. This place had been there many years, and no doubt had seen many weddings, birthdays, and christenings. There was a small kitchen to allow for functions. The wind could be heard outside, whistling around the corrugated tin body and roof. This particular church didn't do the usual prayers and sing-a-longs. There was just a quick blessing, and then straight into the mediumship. I stood up and told a member of the audience, a gentleman, that I had his mother with me.

I was drawn to him. I knew exactly where to go. I said, 'You live on your own in a flat.' He said yes. Amazed by this, I said, 'I've got your mother here, and she is saying to you, have you forgotten where the vacuum cleaner cupboard is?' He laughed, and so did the rest of the congregation. He was well-known, clearly. I said, 'I can see a sink in your kitchen. You need to do the washing up. It is full of plates.' I said, 'There is a big blue plate sticking out of your sink.'

He gasped and laughed. 'Yes,' he said, 'there is.'

'I know. I can see it,' I said. 'You like wildlife, as I can see lots of bird feeders just outside in the garden.'

He agreed. 'Yes, I do.'

I said, 'You read the papers. You don't only read the paper, you read every word, including every advert. You certainly get your money's worth.'

'Yes, you're right. I do.'

'I know. I can see you doing it,' I said. 'And there isn't anything that happens around your home outside without you knowing. I see you are looking around the curtains and know everything that is going on.'

He laughed and said, 'Yes, I do.'

I said, 'I won't say you are nosy. You just know what's going on.' I got this man down to a T. His mother was showing me everything from the spirit world. I said, 'You're not eating properly. That microwave is not the answer to your meals. Your mother showed me that you should get cooking properly, and if you make too much of something, then put it in the fridge for another day. However, don't leave it too long, or it will go off.'

This was a great source of amusement for him. However, he knew I was right. How could I know this? I had never seen him before and never been in his home. I had his mother with me, without a doubt.

When you first start learning to be a medium and you're ready to go out, you start by being a fledgling. You're with a medium who is established, who takes most of the service, and then you stand up and give one or two readings yourself. I only did this three or four times and realised that I didn't need to be there, as I could have taken the whole service on my own. I think this annoyed a few mediums, as they had thought, *He won't be able to do this. He's a new boy. Who does he think he is?* Well, when you've got it, you've got it.

I know this sounds a little bit look-at-me, but what I'm trying to say is that not everybody has to go through the same process, struggling to be able to stand up and give accurate messages. Some people are naturals, and I feel that's that. I have a natural ability, and I know for sure that there are many more of you out there reading this that can do exactly the same. You already get messages. You already see Spirit. You know things are going to happen before they do. You know who is on the phone when it rings. You already have the ability..

When I'm giving readings to people, I've found they expect their life stories. This is not always possible, as you're working with a communicator from the spirit world who will give you specific information to communicate to the recipient. This could sometimes be a short message, where the recipient might be worried about something and the communicator has an answer for him or her. It's not always long and drawn out, but often quite brief. It's down to the medium in many cases to interpret the symbols shown by the communicator. I'm fortunate, as I also see a film running in front of me, which gives me extra help in translating what I'm being shown.

Sometimes the link from the spirit world might not be strong, and sometimes several people may be trying to come through at the same time, which can confuse the message that you try to receive and make you look less competent than you really are. It happens, and it's not your fault, nor that of the communicator—just a lot happening at once.

I was giving a reading to a lady one day, and I said to her that I was being shown a Cornish pasty and brown sauce. I asked if this meant anything, and the reply was, 'I don't believe it. My daughter and I have just had a Cornish pasty with brown sauce before we came out of the house.'

I said, 'Good.' How could I have known this? I also said that I'd been shown a daisy chain.

The lady let out a gasp. She said, 'We have just come from the cemetery, where we have put a daisy chain on the grave.'

I get this all the time. This was undisputed evidence that I had a link with Spirit. It makes me feel good, and most importantly, it makes my recipient feel good that I have a link with his or her loved one in the spirit world. This reading ended on a high note, as always.

I have found over the years that spirits work with me differently than how they did at the beginning of my journey. They show me symbols and I have to interpret the meanings. Sometimes it's a challenge to understand what they're saying to me and what they are trying to show me.

I remember giving a reading to a lady, and she said to me, 'Will I change my car?'

I said, 'Yes. I can see your car being changed from a Volvo to an estate-type car.'

She seemed to look puzzled.

'I can see it happening,' I said to her.

She said, 'I don't think so, as I have cancer and will not be around much longer.' What I had in fact seen was her relatives trading her car for something else.

Another thing I seem to get right, most of the time, is the sex of a baby. One thing we shouldn't do in mediumship is predict the future. However, I'm often clearly shown a baby in a blue ribbon or a pink ribbon. On one occasion I remember giving a reading to a young lady, and I said, 'I'm in the kitchen and it is getting light outside. I can see through the window. There is a tall thermos flask on the side. However, I'm lying on the floor. There are checked tiles, black and white, beneath me.'

She said, 'Yes. I know this. My ex-boyfriend's dad was making his flask one morning in his kitchen, as you described. It was getting light. He was going to work when he had a heart attack and fell on the floor of black and white tiles.'

I also said, 'An ambulance was called. I can see them trying to revive him.'

She said, 'Yes, that's what happened. However, I feel it was too late. He passed.'

There is always a message like this when someone comes through from the spirit world for the recipient. The message here was to look after herself and enjoy life properly. He was clearly fond of her, and he was showing that life on the earth plane can end suddenly and without warning.

31

FRED WEST

I was recently conducting a reading for someone who I've read for on several occasions, and it was apparent that this person in her younger days had been in contact with Fred West, the notorious British murderer who had kidnapped, tortured, raped, and abused young girls for many years and been captured with his wife, Rose. This was probably the biggest case of child abduction and murder the UK has ever seen. Apparently they'd lived in various parts of the country and committed the evil crimes wherever they were, and unfortunately the area around Herefordshire was one of their hunting grounds.

They would drive around in a car offering lifts to lone girls, and then they would be taken away and never seen again. During this reading I was giving the lady, I saw a path along the side of a road with woods to the left of it, and at the end of this path there was a streetlight and a telephone box. I told her that she had been walking along this path when a car stopped and tried to get her to climb inside. She'd refused and run off to this telephone box. The car drove away. She said, 'Yes, that's exactly what happened. It was a yellow three-wheeler car, and at the phone box was a young Gypsy boy I knew.' On seeing him, Fred West had driven off. How lucky was she.

I continued with the reading and said, 'I can see a barn, a black barn on the side of the wood, and that this was just off the main road in a field. Horrible things happened in that barn.' I was then shown the wood behind the barn, and I was shown hessian sacks. This was a barn used by Fred West, and it was clear that these victims had been put in hessian sacks in his vehicle for disposal. It was shown to me that a dog had to be used to find these bodies. This area was near where the attempted abduction had taken place. There had been a book written on this subject, apparently, which I have not read. This information was given to me from the spirit world after Fred and Rose West's arrest.

Fred West died in prison by hanging. Rose West is still alive and still in prison. Unfortunately, surviving family members, of victims which there are a few, have got to live with this horrible story.

Apparently Fred met Rose when she was very young and attractive and introduced her to prostitution at their home. They had a special room constructed with a bar to entertain the clients. However, whilst Rose was entertaining a client, Fred would be watching from a concealed observation point. The police also found in the cellar of their home in Cromwell Street, Gloucester, a bed frame where victims had been tied and abused. This was truly a sick pair of individuals. It is written in Spiritualism that retribution will come to all good and bad deeds committed on the earth plane. Let's hope it does.

It is not known how many victims Fred West had. He would bury them in his garden and under the patio, and several were found in the walls of the house and in fields around Herefordshire and possibly beyond. Who knows? Some have been found. This proves how many runaways were the victims of Fred West. People that had long disappeared, their families thinking that they had left upset with them and never wanted to see them again, had only become victims of this couple. Their families will never know.

However, it is a fact that if it weren't for the Gypsy boy at the phone box, Fred would have definitely had another victim. It makes you wonder how many Fred Wests there are in the world when you hear and watch television programmes on missing teenagers and young adults and see the parents pleading with them to come around—maybe they can't. Recently there was the horror of the case in America, where several young women were held captive in a cellar for ten years. Everyone thought they'd run away or been lost forever. No one knew what the story was until one of them managed to get out of the basement and attract the attention of someone outside. The man that did this was captured and admitted it, which saved a trial and the victims reliving the whole event. However, he will never see daylight in freedom, and again justice prevailed.

Talking of justice in England, we do not have the death penalty, which I'm glad of not because people do not deserve to pay for their sins, no matter how horrendous, but just because it has been proven that they don't always have the right person for the crime. Can you imagine being in this situation, where you look like the perpetrator and were in the area at the time quite innocently, but fit into the frame nicely, and are sentenced to death for something you didn't do? No one will listen no matter what you say. Of course you didn't do it. But you are going to die, so you would say that, wouldn't you?

However, if you wrongly put a person in prison, he or she is still alive, at least, and the person who did it will do it again and again but eventually will be caught, proving the person in prison not guilty. He or she will then be released from jail and hopefully compensated for this miscarriage of justice. Lawyers would be around you like flies trying to take your case, but you would still be alive. Isn't it better than the death penalty? I know the reason the death penalty is called for—because some crimes are so horrendous, especially against children. Public outcry wins the day.

That's why we don't have a death penalty, and in a civilised society it's better to put these people somewhere safe, because to commit these crimes they clearly have severe mental illness. That would be a nice thought to think, that all the world could take this attitude and stop punishing people in this horrible way. I remember seeing on the television recently a child who had allegedly stolen a loaf of bread, then had his arm placed across the curb of the road and a lorry driven over it as punishment. Where does it say in any Bible that you should do this? It's madness. That child was properly starving. Where has the compassion gone in the world? Where does it say that people should act like animals and do what they do to people in some countries, 'in the name of religion'? It is so sad to see this.

32

THE PASSING OF MY PARENTS

My father had a knee operation in his late seventies that involved an anaesthetic. The operation supposedly went well. Unfortunately, he had a mild stroke whilst under the anaesthetic. It was apparent after his operation that he was not how he had been before, so it took a long time to recover, and he did not recover properly. But to my amazement, after suffering as he did, he went back to hospital only a couple of years later and had the other knee done. I said at the time that this was madness; this would not go well. And it didn't. Another stroke happened whilst he was under the anaesthetic. He was not well at all. He started going downhill fast and had no interest in life, and it was apparent something was seriously wrong.

He refused to take his medication and refused to eat and drink. He was taken into hospital in Cambridge, England. I went to visit him,. I told him to get out of that bed. *You can do it. You can walk.* It was as if he had given up on life. He got very aggressive with my mother. Threats of violence towards her were not good. I went on holiday to France. I was in Brest when I received a telephone call from my mother. 'Dad's not good,' she said. I knew by her tone and voice that I should come home.

I said to her, 'Should I be there?'

She said, 'Well, yes.'

I returned to Cambridge and visited the hospital to find that he'd been transferred to another room. It was apparent why he was in that room. The nurse attending him was asked by my mother if he wanted a drink of alcohol could he have it? The reply had been yes, to give him whatever he wanted. I knew there was no hope and that he was about to return to the spirit world.

I phoned my eldest brother and told him to get to the hospital, as I didn't think Dad would last until tomorrow. My words were not taken seriously. Visiting time was eleven o'clock the following day. I said we should all go and see him, and we arrived at ten thirty. There is a small cafeteria in the reception area of this hospital where we sat until eleven. Then we proceeded to the ward—my mother, my eldest brother, my partner, and I. As I walked along the ward to the room, the nurse in charge said to us, 'I have been trying to contact you. Your father has just passed away.'

There he was lying in the bed, and it was obvious to us all that he had not just passed. He had been gone awhile, you could see. He looked so small and feeble lying there. I remember my brother said, 'That's not my dad.' I looked at him and agreed that this big, strong person that we knew was now a shadow of his former self. I remember my mother not kissing him, as you would expect, but she put two fingers together, kissed them, and touched his head. That was it. We left the room.

How did I feel? Well I suppose many people get upset, cry, never get over it. I won't say that, as I have become cold towards death from my life's journey, and I certainly know that I did not have the feelings that many would in this situation; as I have said before, my upbringing was not the best, as violence was always there with my parents.

I remember my father punching me full in the face, hard, when I was only about fifteen, for arriving home half an hour late one evening. I knew at the time he'd been wound up by my mother. Nevertheless, he still did it, and maybe that was still in my memory. I always feel that if you can't handle what life throws at you and you have children, don't take it out on them. Let someone else bring them up. I wish that had been my case. All I wanted was loving parents, but that never happened.

My mother was now on her own. My youngest brother, who used to work for the Inland Revenue, Customs and Excise, VAT, looked after her financial affairs because he knew the system, in his own words; we were never a close family, which is simply to say that we didn't see eye to eye with one another. It was always who was better than who, especially in my parents' eyes. My parents had moved to sheltered accommodation approximately eight years before my father's passing. It was not a good move, as it was a very small one-bedroom apartment on the ground floor without a garden. I tried to advise against it, but they wouldn't listen. They sold the house to move there. I suppose it was all about money.

My mother visited my house in Hereford at Christmas. She was hard work. I suppose I invited her through duty. Anyway, it was thrown back at me. The following year my youngest brother decided that he would have her at Christmas with him. At the time I thought the duty of having my mother it should be shared among the family, as she was a responsibility; what I did not know was that he had my mother's accounts, so there were other motives. My mother finally said one day that she'd been to the hospital, as she had lumps in her stomach. All was not well. She had cancer.

Things weren't good for her—a lot of pain and suffering. I went to visit her, and you could see she was not good. My youngest brother was there like some guard dog. Why all the sudden interest? This had never happened before. There were problems with her illness that required assistance in even the basic daily chores, including sanitary. My younger brother helped her but moaned about it behind her back. I'm sure this must have been embarrassing for her. However, he did it all the same.

Once when I visited her in the flat, my eldest brother arrived. These two did not see eye to eye in any way whatsoever. There was always aggression between them and threats of violence, which my youngest brother always said would be answered by the authorities, the police. All wasn't well while we were there. A letter arrived. My mother said, 'What is that?' to my youngest brother, who had already opened it. He said, 'It's from the solicitor. Don't worry. I'll talk to you about it later.' He was handling all of her financial affairs.

I went into the toilet, sat down, and tried to get a link with my father, and yes, he came through—the brightest picture I've ever seen. He told me to go to the shop and get a dozen red roses, and even showed me the red roses. These were bright red roses. And he said, 'I will be along in six weeks to fetch her.'

I told my two brothers who were out of earshot of my mother what had just happened in the toilet. My youngest brother said, 'Yes, that would go with what the doctors have told me.' I then went to the local supermarket, to the flower stall inside, and there, to my surprise, was a bunch of bright red roses just as I'd been shown—just one bunch.

I purchased them and returned to my mother's flat. I didn't tell her what had happened. Sometime after this meeting my mother deteriorated fast. My youngest brother moved her to his house. He wouldn't let her out of his sight. No one was allowed to go and get her to take her out. He did everything himself. I went to Cambridge to see her again. It wasn't good. You could see that she was soon to go back to the spirit world. Her eyes had gone just as my father's had, and she had a very miserable look on her face, which I'd seen before. She passed in his house some days later.

The funeral took place a week or so later. She had requested to be cremated as my father had. My father said in his own words, when asked what he wanted done with his ashes, to just chuck them around the roses at the crematorium. It was like we were being told that his life was nothing and that he thought nothing of it. I don't know what happened to my mother's ashes. I was never told.

This wasn't the end but only the beginning of the problems. Any one of you who has been unfortunate enough to experience bereavement of a relative like this will know that there is a terrible thing in this world called greed. And yes, it happened here. What we didn't know was that the will had been made and that my eldest brother and I were left with £2000 each, and my youngest brother would have what was remaining in her account for his efforts.

What we also didn't know was that my aunt, who was in fact my god-mother, had passed some months before and left my mother £170,000 in her will. My youngest brother knew about this; in fact, the letter from the solicitor was to inform my mother of it. This would have changed a lot of things, as I'm sure if she had known about this money it would have been split three ways, but it wasn't. My youngest brother put it into the bank account he controlled for my mother. He gave my brother and I the £2000 stated in the will and kept the rest for himself, openly boasting about this to me. He said, 'After you had your money, whatever was left was mine.' Greed, indeed.

I know for a fact that this is not an isolated case. I know of other people that produced wills that hadn't existed before and now suddenly do on passing, all for financial gain—not good. One of the seven principles of Spiritualism is compensation and retribution hereafter for all the good and evil deeds done on Earth.

My mother has come through on readings that I have done several times since she has passed, and I've asked her why she treated me like she did. She said, 'Get over it,' like it was nothing, like it hadn't happened. When she came through I saw her lying on a sun bed being waited on by fit young men wearing just white shorts. She had on a white bikini. Clearly her body had reverted back to her early twenties. She was lapping up the sun and the attention. I asked her if she had seen my father. She said, 'He's off doing what he does.' By this I can only assume she meant womanising; apparently he had an interest in this whilst on the earth plane. I feel this could have been part of the problem. Unfortunately, this would be taken out on everyone around her. I suppose it is something people do when they can't hit back.

33

PSYCHOMETRY

This is the psychic ability to pick up an object and tell things about its owner through the energy of the person who owned it before. . One love in my life is playing the guitar, and I started in the 1960s when bands like the Beatles were around. I don't know whether it was an urge to be noticed or the love of bands; however, guitar has been one of my loves. This came to a point only a few years ago, when I recorded sixteen tracks in a full studio of Hank Marvin's *From the Shadows* CD. I played lead guitar and learned all of these tracks. I must say I was pleased with my efforts. It took two years of practice to learn this with no prior musical training classes, which was a good achievement.

A friend of mine who lives in London visited me for a couple of days with his son, and he brought with him his guitar. His son also had one. We were playing together for a while one evening and having a good time with lots of smiles, as we all knew the same songs, when he said to me, 'What do you think of this one?' He had an old, battered, hard guitar case placed in a corner. He said that I should have a look, so I did. On opening the case, there inside was a very old Gibson guitar. He told me that this was a prototype. I did not doubt him whatsoever. It must have been worth a lot of money.

He told me to take it out and look at it, and as I did, I said, 'Wow. I can see a man and a girl. Someone has taken someone's life.' And I went on to give a full description of what I saw. I looked at them and they were sitting there grinning at each other. I was spot-on. In fact, this had been owned by a friend of his who had murdered someone and been incarcerated for a number of years because of it.

I asked how he had come by the guitar, and he said that he had gone to visit the owner in prison, who had asked him to clean out his place. He mentioned his guitars asked if he would sell them for him and have the pick of any that he wanted. My friend took the Gibson. What a choice. This was my first big psychometry reading, and I got it right the first time. We have these gifts we don't know about. I was very pleased, and I've done it many times since and given very accurate information to the recipients—of course helped by the spirit world, I have no doubt at all.

The fact of picking up an object and giving a story like that I find amazing. It just comes to me and I see it. If you look on some of the programmes on television on the Discovery Channel, you will see psychics being used by the police in America, giving information most accurately about a murder and seeing who did it, the car that was used, the weapon, the relationship to the victim. This all comes through, even the location of the deceased.

I was sitting with a group of friends one evening recently and the subject of psychics came up. There were three of us sitting around the table who I knew well, and one not so well. This person said to me that his wife was very interested in the abilities of psychic mediums. I said, 'Yes, we are fortunate,' and with this he produced a plastic bag from his pocket, took a medal like a coin out, and gave it to me.

'Tell me what you can get out of this,' he said. I knew it was a test. This often happens. Without looking at the object, I asked where he had come by this. He said, 'I have a metal detector and I found it recently with some others. What do you get from it?'

I saw straightaway and I said, 'I see a field like an arena. There are people running around in white shorts. There is a line round this arena. I also see Roman shields and spears and Roman sandals. I'm also picking up Viking ships and longboats.'

He came back to me and said, 'I found this coin on a football field by a Roman road that used to be the area of a massive Roman settlement.' There was a computer turned on in the corner of the room, and he showed me where the site was. It was right by the sea—hence me seeing the long-boats—and there was a football field where he had found the coin, and right on the edge of the football field was a straight road, a Roman road.

He said, 'Three out of three.' I was very pleased, as I'd been tested by a nonbeliever and come through with colours blazing. Yes, I have confidence in my ability, and of course it's the spirit world that showed me everything I told him. Thank you, Spirit, once again.

Unfortunately, there is a lot of scepticism in the world with regard to psychic abilities, and unfortunately the charlatans give us a bad name. If people have experienced them, then as far as they are concerned, we are all the same. As you know from reading this book, that is not the case. There are people out there with true abilities, wonderful abilities, able to speak to the spirit world and receive communication from them, proving that we don't die. Life doesn't just end. We are spirit people having an earthly experience, and one day we will return to the spirit world more the wiser for our experiences. Clearly we must pass tests to go on with our spirit lives.

You as the reader can try psychometry yourself. When you are at a friend's house, say to him or her that you are trying to learn psychometry and see if it works. Ask for something from a relative that you can hold in your hand, only a small object like a ring or a watch or some other piece of property owned by someone else. Hold it in your hands, both hands grasped together, and see what you see. Keep it there for a while. What can you see? Do you get the vision of a person? Can you see an event or situation? Do you get a name? Tell the person who gave the object what you're seeing and ask for confirmation. You will be surprised, as you may well have the ability to do psychometry. Keep practising and it will progress. Also, make sure that you are sitting in a quiet place without a lot of noise around you, as otherwise you will be distracted and unable to concentrate. Good luck.

34

MY MUSICAL INTERESTS

One of the loves in my life has been music. . I'm a self-taught guitarist and have also played guitar in a rock band. I enjoy music, as it's a way of relaxing. It takes the strain of the day away but can involve hard studying. It's always been with me, the wanting to play guitar. I grew up in the sixties, when bands or groups, as we called them then, were starting, like the Beatles and the Rolling Stones and many more. These were the pioneers. Today we must thank them for their contribution. I remember I'd watch them on the television and wish it could be me. I knew I could do that, and I would have loved to be up there in the lights. It was exciting and fun.

I've always had a guitar. I own at least three. One of my favourite guitarists is Hank Marvin from the Shadows. I wished for years that I could play like him, and a couple of years ago I got my wish. I set myself the task of learning his tunes on the lead guitar. I purchased a Fender Stratocaster in salmon pink, just like Hank's. I changed the pickups to Kinmans, just like Hank uses, and I had the tremolo arm changed by the same man who does Hank's guitars. I purchased a guitar effects unit like the one used by Hank Marvin, and I got all the backing tracks that I wanted to record onto a CD. These were available without the lead guitar, in which I would play on my guitar.

I spent two years studying. I bought his DVDs and all his CDs. I studied them and studied him. It drove people mad listening to me on the guitar playing Hank Marvin, but I would practice every day, and when I got up in the morning, I would pick up the guitar again and see if I could remember what I had learnt the night before. I always could. Then I searched for a recording studio, as I was determined to make a CD, and I found one. Off I went to play Hank Marvin. It took twelve weeks, on and off, to record sixteen tracks. I remember the technician saying to me, 'You must be pretty confident to be able to come here and want to make music like this.'

I was determined to finish this work, and I kept at it until finally the CD was complete. The technician enquired if I had a name for it, and I said yes: *Bob Plays Hank*.

When I play it now, I think of all the hard work that went into it and how hard I would have to work to try to recreate it again, as it's one of those things: if you don't play guitar on a regular basis, you lose it. And I put in some very hard tunes, like the theme from *The Deer Hunter*, 'Don't Cry for Me, Argentina,' and the themes from *Titanic* and *Apache*. One of the tunes that I tried hardest on and have always wanted to play was the theme from *Local Hero*, 'Going Home.'

It just proves that if you want something bad enough, you can get it, and in this case I feel it was a lifetime achievement. Once again, thank you,

Spirit. You gave me the drive and determination, as always, to carry on and achieve once again, for me, the near impossible.

I would encourage anyone to learn a musical instrument. I wish that I would have had the opportunity at a younger age to play guitar, with people who were already accomplished, as this would have brought me on a lot quicker, and a lot of the struggling I had to do would have been easier. You learn from others, and I think this is important, especially with bands. If you have a very good guitarist, he can show the others what to do and what part to play. This speeds up the process and helps to keep it 'tight'; this is the musician's word for 'together.'

Once again, where does this determination come from? Well, it's quite simple. We are guided by spirits. We are helped in our achievements by those who have gone before us. Drive and determination are what is required to achieve the near impossible. It can be done, and on a regular basis, as anyone will know who has done well in business. No one gives it to you; it's hard work, long hours, and sacrifices. However, you will achieve your aim. It's good to be at the top, most of the time.

The summer music festivals in England, and the most famous of all being Glastonbury. Glastonbury is a magical place, with a very long spiritual history. You must visit this town and go into the shops and meet the people. You can't help but be touched by the friendliness. I didn't see one policeman on my last trip to Glastonbury town, as there is no need. The shops are something else. They are a spiritual heaven. I urge you to go there as part of your journey, and to go to the festival.

The Rolling Stones were centre stage at Glastonbury in 2013 and still rocking into their seventies.

If you intend to get into music or have a child who is interested, my best advice is to simply buy them the best equipment you can afford. It doesn't have to be brand-new. eBay and other places like this can often save you a lot of money when looking for equipment, compared with the shop prices.

The results will come straightaway. The smile on your son or daughter's face will be worth it when they start making the tunes all on their own. And remember, whatever your age, you are never too old to learn. It's there for you if you want to take the challenge. Also remember that Spirit will be with you all the way; you're not on your own.

This is Bob with his first guitar, notice it's home-made. He had a flair from a young age of music.

My Guitar

When I strum my guitar, my mind wanders far.
Some call it an axe, but it helps me relax.
It's made up of sharps and flats
and scales that help you play
in your own special way.
Music is my escape every day.
You too should learn to play.

You have to keep it in tune.
Start with a low E and then an A.
D follows soon. So does G. Get it in tune.
And B after that. Make sure it's not flat.
And finally the high E, and you're away.
Test your rig and you're ready to gig.

Learn chords to the songs.
You mustn't get them wrong
or it won't sound right
and you'll be practising all night.
Do it again and again until it sounds the same.
Listen to the song.
It will help you play along
and help you sound the same.
Well, that is your aim.
Play rhythm. Play lead.
Learn it at your own speed.
Take away the book.
You don't need to look.

The Psychic Soldier

You'll get there now on your own.
Your confidence has grown.

Listen to a tune. Play with the chords.
You'll get it soon.
Is it in E, or maybe G?
Try the sequence and you will see.
The lead can be found in the scales around.
Change the key. It works for me.

I love my guitar. It takes me far.
Happiness is found when the strap is wrapped round
your body, you see.
Look at me. I can play the guitar.
I worked hard to get this far, but look at me now.
You wish you knew how.
When you see, take a tip from me.
Hard work always pays.
That's why I can play in this special way.

35

SUMMARY

My life has been a strange journey, but I have memories, very good memories, of every stage, and I know that it is very unusual for someone who started his life out as I did, with no hope of the future, worrying whether I would see the next day and not accepting the words of critics, especially my mother. I fought on. I was not going to be beaten. I had determination and the willpower to succeed, to not accept that this was my lot. I went out into the world on my own to better myself, to get myself a better life. Yes, I made mistakes on the way. Don't we all? Did I achieve my ambition? I think so.

It's funny, though; I always felt I could have done better, and I could have achieved more. I would have liked to learn to fly. I have flown several helicopters, obviously supervised. It's just a nice thing to have done. I think looking for the freedom of the skies ties to Spirit, which is with me now every day, and I'm pleased I found it, or it found me. You need to experience this. It is good for you, as far as I know. I'm the only person to have achieved all this—by this I mean gone through the military like I did to be involved in conflicts and then to find Spirit. I wouldn't have had it any other way.

Having said this, I would have liked a better upbringing. I see people who think the world of their parents, something I never had, but I'm not sad about this now, as I've got Spirit and I can communicate whenever I want. I can sit with people and tell them things that I couldn't possibly have known. I see full-body apparitions around me. I noticed only today a new building that I once gave a lady a reading about. I told her that her boss was going to build a state-of-the-art building and that people would go there for special treatment and care. I described it. I passed that place today, and next to the building where she previously worked was this brand-new one. Spirit showed me this. How could I have known? It just shows and proves beyond doubt that we have a link with the spirit world and can communicate. They talk to us and show us the future. This proves it. They are there for us. You should talk to them. Sit in a quiet room and ask them, 'What should I do? Show me.' And they will. You don't have to talk out loud. You can do this without speaking. Just think of the thought, and you will be surprised at the results.

Spirit Is with Me

Spirit is with me day and night. I know it is there, so when I see it,
it doesn't give me a fright.
Why be afraid when you see it near?
It is probably somebody that you love dear.
There are many spirit people that I would love to come near,
good friends that I have lost over many a year.

Each night when I get ready to sleep,
I ask Spirit for my safety to keep,
and to please let me wake up the following day,
as I have work to do, no time to play.

I asked spirit to keep me going for many a year,
as I have work to do that won't finish here.
I always asked spirit to guide me through life,
keep me on the straight and narrow, and show me a light,
so that I may guide others who wish to communicate with the afterlife.

I asked spirit to help people see good,
stop the wars and the killing, and practice brotherhood.
People are here to learn lessons, that I know.
Why so much suffering?
Just to show
mistakes that they make.
I wish that they all would take a break
before the world disappears in some massive earthquake.

I'm glad I found spirit, or it found me. We make a good partnership, as
you can see.

257

I like writing poetry. You must try it yourself. You will be surprised at the outcome, and it is also uplifting, as you have achieved something that you never knew you could. I found this with my first poem, 'Gallant Men.'

Do I have ambitions in life? Mainly I love reading to people and communicating with the spirit world, bringing the two worlds closer together, proving that we don't just die; we live on. Our spirits go back to the spirit world, and we become once again spirit people, as we always have been. Remember, these are earthly bodies. We are having an earthly experience. We will go back to the spirit world and live on forever. We will be reunited with our loved ones, so don't fear death; it is merely the end of our time on earth, where we will live forever and thereafter in the spirit world.

And yes, we can come back and communicate with our loved ones. We can appear to them as our loved ones appear to us. We will be able to leave white feathers, to show that we have visited and be there in times of sadness for those left behind.

I meet people throughout my life who say they've been dealt a bad hand and there's no hope for them. It might be where they live, or the circumstances surrounding them. They have no work. Life is just another day with no hope for them. Well, I can say there are two things needed in life: belief in yourself and determination. The will to win.

With this the unachievable can be achieved. Spirit is with you, guiding you and helping you all the way. You need to believe, and you can achieve. Thank you for reading this book, and I hope that it has helped many of you. It shows that there is hope for everyone. Just believe.

And I wish you all
love and light.

Bob